THE MEASURE OF A

GENE A. GETZ

A Division of GL Publications
Ventura, CA U.S.A.

Other good reading by Gene A. Getz:
The Measure of a Church
The Measure of a Family
The Measure of a Man
The Measure of a Marriage
The Measure of a Christian—Studies in James 1
The Measure of a Christian—Studies in Philippians
The Measure of a Christian—Studies in Titus

The translation of all Regal books is under the direction of GLINT. GLINT provides technical help for the adaptation, translation and publishing of books for millions of people worldwide. For information regarding translation contact: GLINT, P.O. Box 6688, Ventura, California 93006.

Trade Edition, 1984
Twelfth Printing, 1983

Published by Regal Books
A Division of GL Publications
Ventura, California 93006
Printed in U.S.A.

Library of Congress Catalog Card No. 77-074533
ISBN 0-8307-0981-9

A Leader's Guide for use in group study is available from your church supplier.

Contents

To my wife, Elaine, I owe a great tribute for help-ing me get this book ready for publication. Most encouraging to me has been her Christlike example.

Thanks, also, to a number of godly women who serve as wives of elders and deacons at Fellowship Bible Church, and who first studied, evaluated and applied this material. Their comments and ideas have been very helpful in preparing this manuscript for publication.

I would also like to express my personal appreciation to my good friend, Dr. Phil Williams, who evaluated some of the technical facets of this manuscript. Phil teaches New Testament exegesis at Northwest Baptist Seminary in Tacoma, Washington.

WHY THIS STUDY?

Though what Paul and other New Testament writers say about Christian maturity and renewal is equally applicable to both men and women, they did have some special things to say to Christian women and how they can *each* develop and reflect the mind of Christ. This book, therefore, focuses on *personal renewal* for Christian women.

RENEWAL—A BIBLICAL PERSPECTIVE

Renewal is the essence of dynamic Christianity and the basis on which Christians, both in a corporate or Body sense and as individual believers, can determine the will of God. Paul made this clear when he wrote to the Roman Christians—"be transformed by the *renewing of your mind*. Then," he continued, "you will be able to test and approve what God's will is" (Rom. 12:2). Here Paul is talking about renewal in both a personal and a corporate sense. In other words, Paul is asking these Christians as a *body* of believers to develop the mind of Christ through corporate renewal.

Personal renewal will not happen as God intended it

unless it happens in the context of corporate renewal. On the other hand, corporate renewal will not happen as God intended without personal renewal. Both are necessary.

Biblical Renewal

Romans 12:1,2

The larger circle represents "church renewal." This is the most comprehensive concept in the New Testament. However, every local church is made up of smaller self-contained, but interrelated units. The *family* in Scripture emerges as the church in miniature. In turn, the family is made up of an even smaller social unit—*marriage.* The third inner circle represents *personal* renewal, which is inseparably linked to all of the other basic units. Marriage is made up of two separate individuals who become one. The family is made up of parents and children who are also to reflect the mind of Christ. And the church is made up of not only individual Christians, but couples and families.

Though all of these social units are interrelated, biblical renewal can begin within any specific social unit. But wherever it begins—in the church, families, marriages, or individuals—the process immediately touches all the other social units. And one thing is certain! All that God says is consistent and harmonious. He does not have one set of principles for the church and another set for the family, another for husbands and wives and another for individual Christians. For example, the principles God outlines for local church elders, fathers, and husbands regarding their role as leaders are interrelated and consistent. If they are not, we can be sure that we have not interpreted God's plan accurately.

The books listed below are part of the Biblical Renewal Series by Gene Getz designed to provide supportive help in moving toward renewal. They all fit into one of the circles described above and will provoke thought, provide interaction and tangible steps toward growth.

ONE ANOTHER SERIES	*PERSONALITY SERIES*	*THE MEASURE OF SERIES*
Building Up One Another	*Abraham*	*Measure of a . . .*
	David	*Church*
Encouraging One Another	*Joseph*	*Family*
	Joshua	*Man*
	Moses	*Marriage*
Loving One Another	*Nehemiah*	*Woman*
	Elijah	*Christian—*
Serving One Another		*Philippians*
		Christian— Titus
		Christian— James 1

Sharpening the Focus of the Church presents an overall perspective for Church Renewal. All of these books are available from your bookstore.

PREFACE
WHY THIS?

This book, like *The Measure of a Man,* emerged as a result of a process. Once a month, my wife Elaine met with a group of women to study the qualities for measuring the maturity level of a woman. Thirteen characteristics were used from three significant passages of Scripture: 1 Timothy 3:11; Titus 2:3-5; and 1 Peter 3:1-4.

Originally I wrote these studies as open-ended drafts for interaction and discussion, with suggested practical steps for applying these biblical truths. As a result of this process, a number of the women involved in this study added helpful ideas and suggestions to the original materials. Together, Elaine and I have revised and refined these original studies. The result is *The Measure of a Woman.* We trust you'll enjoy studying it as much as we enjoyed the process of putting it together. And more important, our prayer is that this material will continually help you conform your life more and more to the image of Jesus Christ.

Gene A. Getz

INTRODUCTION
HOW TO
USE THIS BOOK

Each chapter in this book is self-contained, presenting a biblical mark or characteristic of Christian maturity for women. At the end of each chapter there are practical steps to assist you in developing this particular quality in your life.

You can study each chapter *on your own* and work out each personal project as you go. Better yet, read it *with your husband* or *a close friend,* and work through the practical steps together.

Or you can combine this approach with a women's study group. Share the leadership responsibilities with the group. Take one chapter for each discussion meeting. Use the book as a springboard into the Scriptures. Discuss your findings. Divide into smaller units, if convenient, and work through the practical steps at the end of each chapter.

A final word! Remember Paul's testimony regarding his own Christian life-style: "Not that I have already obtained all this, or have already been made perfect, but I press on to take hold of that for which Christ Jesus took hold of me. Brothers, I do not consider myself yet to have taken hold of it. But one thing I do: Forgetting what is behind and straining toward what is ahead, I press on toward the goal to win the prize for which God has called me heavenward in Christ Jesus" (Phil. 3:12-14).

1 GOD'S
PERSPECTIVE
ON BEAUTY

"An excellent wife, who can find? For her worth is far above jewels." (Prov. 31:10, NASB)

How do you measure a woman? Her worth, her true beauty, her total being? Historically, it's obvious that the criteria have often been very specific and restrictive. And today's society highlights this narrow point of view by many means. Simply stated, it is physical appearance. Movies, magazines, television, all bear constant witness to this external obsession.

God's perspective on women, however, is far more comprehensive. Obviously, God is not opposed to beauty—not even sensual beauty. In a unique and incomparable way, He created "woman for man" (see 1 Cor. 11:9). And any normal man bears witness to this reality. He responds to what he sees. In fact, the Lord Himself saw that what He had made was "very good" (see Gen. 1:31). Though part of what God saw was physical beauty ("And the man and his wife were both naked and were not ashamed" Gen. 2:25, *NASB*) the most significant qualities

were internal. This is obvious from the rest of Scripture.
Unfortunately, God's intended perspective on women
has been marred. Sin, entering the world, caused man to
focus on external beauty and to abuse it, pervert it and use
it for all kinds of selfish purposes.

But God's perspective goes on nevertheless! And men
and women who seek to do God's will can discover what
that perspective is. It neither eliminates physical beauty,
nor excludes inner qualities. God's perspective certainly
includes both, but puts the emphasis where it ought to
be—on what is real, lasting, and ultimately satisfying—
and all within His moral laws. And this is what this book is
all about. We trust you'll take its message seriously. If you
do, it can help change your life.

The apostle Paul, in stating the qualifications for elder-
ship in 1 Timothy 3 and Titus 1, portrays a dynamic profile
for Christian maturity, not only for men but also for
women. In fact, most of the qualities he lists for men in
these passages are repeated elsewhere in the New Testament for *all* members of the Body of Christ. [1]

But Paul, and also the apostle Peter, specified some
qualities that are uniquely directed at women. These vir-
tues in turn serve as criteria for measuring Christian
maturity and true and lasting beauty.

Note that even though these qualities are specifically
directed at women, just as the qualities in 1 Timothy 3 and
Titus 1 are directed at men, they are often mentioned
elsewhere in the New Testament for all members of the
Body of Christ.

At least three passages stand out boldly in the New
Testament. Though there are qualities that are repeated,
each passage of Scripture also highlights some unique
characteristics for measuring the maturity level of a Christian woman. The number beside each quality indicates the
chapter in this book in which the quality is discussed. [2]

First Timothy 3:11
Wives are to be women![3]
> *Worthy of respect,* (2)
>> *not*
> *malicious talkers,* (3)
>> but
> *temperate* (4)
>> and
> *trustworthy in everything.* (5)

Titus 2:3-5
Likewise, teach the older women to be
> *reverent in the way they live,* (2)
>> *not to be*
> *slanderers* (3)
>> *or*
> *addicted to much wine,* (4)
>> but to
> *teach what is good.* (6)

Then they can train the younger women to
> *love their husbands* (7)
>> and *children,* (8) to be
> *self-controlled* (9) and
> *pure* (10) to be
> *busy at home,* (11) to be
> *kind,* (12)
>> and to be
> *subject to their husbands,* (13)

so that no one will malign the word of God.

First Peter 3:1-4
Wives, in the same way be
> *submissive to your husbands*

so that, if any of them do not believe the word, they may
be won over without talk by the behavior of their wives,
when they see the
purity
and
reverence of your lives.
Your beauty should not come from
outward adornment,
such as braided hair
and the wearing of gold jewelry
and fine clothes.
Instead, it should be that of your inner self, the
unfading beauty of a
gentle and quiet spirit. (14)
These Scripture passages form the basis for this
study. Each yields several significant aspects that reflect
qualities of inner beauty. Down deep they represent what
all human beings (men particularly) desire to see in a
woman. In fact, without them, physical beauty is merely
temporary and superficial. With them, even what some
consider to be physical inadequacies are overshadowed by
what is ultimately meaningful and endearing.

Footnotes

1. See Gene A. Getz, *The Measure of a Man* (Ventura: Regal Books, 1974).
2. The arrangement of the mechanical outline in these Scripture passages is
based on logic and concept relationships, rather than strict rules of grammar.
3. Italics added. Hereafter all italics in Scripture quotations are added by the
author.

2 TO BE WORTHY
OF RESPECT

"In the same way, their wives are to be women worthy of respect." (1 Tim. 3:11)

There is a difference of opinion regarding what Paul had in mind when he referred to women in 1 Timothy 3:11. In the *King James Version* and the *New International Version,* the translators use the word "wives." The word in the *New American Standard Bible* is translated "women." And Williams used the word "deaconesses." The fact is, it is difficult to know what word is best except by the total context.

It is really not terribly significant what word is used because it is clear from the context of 1 Timothy 3:11 that Paul is discussing the marks of maturity for a Christian woman—whether she is married or whether she is not; whether she has an official position in the church or whether she does not. In fact, the most universal meaning of the Greek word *gunee* refers to a woman of any age, whether single, married or a widow.

Personally, I feel the English word "women" is the

best translation. Otherwise, Paul would be outlining qualifications for the "wives" of deacons without saying anything about the "wives" of elders. If this were true, it would seem to be a significant omission since serving as an elder's (or pastor's) wife is usually more demanding than serving as a deacon's wife. This is assuming, of course, that the men filling these offices are functioning according to biblical specifications.[1]

It seems more logical, then, to conclude that Paul first spelled out the qualifications of elders (see 1 Tim. 3:1-7). Then he delineated the qualifications for *men* who were to serve in the church as deacons (see 1 Tim. 3:8-10), quickly followed by the qualifications for *women* who were likewise to occupy *serving* positions. Thus the word "deaconesses" as used by Williams in his translation seems to get at the basic meaning of what Paul had in mind. While the New Testament clearly states or implies that elders are to be men (see 1 Tim. 3:1-7; Titus 1:5-9), it in no way eliminates women from serving others in the church. For example, consider Euodia and Syntyche (see Phil. 4:2), and Priscilla, the wife of Aquila (see Rom. 16:3), and Lydia in Philippi (see Acts 16:14).

August, Venerable, Reverent, Honorable

One of the qualities of maturity specified by Paul in 1 Timothy 3:11 is that the person be "worthy of respect." The basic Greek word is *semnos,* meaning "august, venerable, reverent, honorable." Here Paul is talking about a woman who lives in such a way that she can be "venerated for her character." However, Paul also mentions this quality for men.

Paul used the same basic word to describe the maturity level of deacons. They, too, were to be "worthy of respect" *(NIV)* or "men of *dignity*" (1 Tim. 3:8, *NASB*).

Older men should have this quality. Paul again used the

basic word *semnos* when writing to Titus to exhort him to also encourage older men to be *"dignified" (NASB)* and "worthy of respect" (Titus 2:2, *NIV*).

Paul described the goal that all Christians should have for their lives. He exhorted all believers to pray "for kings and all who are in authority in order that we may lead a tranquil and quiet life in all godliness and *dignity*"[2] (2 Tim. 2:2, *NASB*). Here the word is used along with the word "godliness," or that which reflects God's character.

Pastors and teachers should manifest this quality. Paul used this Greek word with special reference to *how* different people should teach the Word of God. His specific exhortation was to Titus, a New Testament pastor and teacher in Crete. "In all things show yourself to be an example of good deeds, with purity in doctrine, *dignified,* sound in speech which is beyond reproach, in order that the opponent may be put to shame, having nothing bad to say about us" (Titus 2:7,8, *NASB*).

Williams translated this concept even more pointedly, demonstrating how the message we teach is enhanced and made more effective by our own personality: "In everything you yourself continue to set them a worthy example of doing good; be sincere and *serious* in your teaching, let your message be wholesome and unobjectionable, so that our opponent may be put to shame at having nothing evil to say about us."[3]

The whole tone of this exhortation is that we should teach carefully and in a dignified way. Putting it in twentieth-century language, we must make sure we have carefully researched what we teach; our interpretations and applications should be accurate, and we should teach with confidence blended with humility and sincerity. Then, Paul says, we will impress even those who do not believe God's Word.

The same exhortation applies to women in leadership

roles. As we will see in future chapters, this type of "respectful" life-style is particularly important for "older" women who are teaching "younger" women how to live the Christian life in their various relationships. In fact, Paul exhorted Titus to "teach the older women to be *reverent in the way they live* . . . . Then they [will be able to] train the younger women" to live with their husbands and children in such a way so *"that no one will malign the word of God"* (Titus 2:3-5). This Pauline concern, of course, correlates with what he wrote to Titus in Titus 2:7,8. A respectable, reverent, and dignified life-style (whether pastor or teacher or general Christian) will form a backdrop against which the opponents of Christianity "may be ashamed because they have nothing bad to say about us" (Titus 2:8).

The World of Ideas and Things

There is another use of *semnos* in the New Testament that is significant in developing the quality of respect and dignity in our lives. It has to do with what we think about—the world of "ideas" and "things." Thus Paul wrote to the Philippians: "Finally, brethren, . . . whatever is *honorable* [worthy of respect] . . . let your mind dwell on these things" (Phil. 4:8, *NASB*).

We cannot expect others to respect us if we think about things that are dishonorable or disrespectful. We cannot even develop *self*-respect this way, and without self-respect, we cannot win the respect of others. We read in Proverbs, As a man "thinketh in his heart, so is he" (Prov. 23:7, *KJV*). What are things that a woman can think about and do that could cause her to lose self-respect and consequently the respect of others?

Literature, television shows, movies—anything that stimulates carnal appetites and that focuses on non-Christian behavior will eventually affect our self-respect. Many modern-day novels, magazine articles, and soap operas cater to the flesh and focus on lying, cheating, illegitimate sex, backbiting, gossiping, foul language, etc. Any Christian woman who takes seriously God's standards for living, yet allows her mind to "think on these things" will sooner or later lose self-respect and be in danger of losing the respect of her husband, her children and her close friends.

A Personal or Group Project

The following personal project is designed to help you as a Christian woman develop self-respect as well as respect from others.

Step A: Honestly ask yourself, "What about me indicates that I have self-respect?"

1. Do I feel good about myself?

Note: Self-respect is not pride. The Bible says we are to love our neighbor as ourselves (see Lev. 19:18). There is a "self-love" that is biblically and psychologically proper. Without it we neither win the respect of others nor ourselves.

2. What evidence do I have that other people respect me? If single, my male companions? If married, my husband and children? My close friends? Other members of the Body of Christ?

Important: How you feel about yourself is not necessarily an indication of how others feel about you. "Lack of self-respect" and an "inferiority complex" are not necessarily synonymous. In other words, you may "look in the mirror" and feel bad about yourself. But others may view you as a very good person. At this point, either you are being deceitful in your life before others or your view of yourself is incorrect. Which is it?

Step B: To determine whether or not your view of yourself is related to an inferiority complex or valid feelings of personal disrespect, ask yourself: Are there any attitudes and actions in my life that are in direct violation of Scripture? Do I have a moral problem? Am I a bitter person? Am I proud and arrogant? Am I gossiping about others?

If your answer is yes to any of these questions, this may be why you don't respect yourself. However, if you are doing all you know how to do to live a good Christian life and still feel like an inferior person, then your problem is no doubt more psychological than spiritual.

Note: If it is psychological in nature, it may be manifesting itself as a spiritual problem but in its root it is still psychological and must be dealt with at that level.

Feelings of inferiority and discomfort will inevitably create spiritual problems. But to deal with these problems on a purely spiritual level may actually accentuate the problem and make you feel worse.

Note: If there is no flagrant sin in your life, and if other people view you with respect, then your negative feelings about yourself are no doubt psychological in nature.

Step C: Now that you have isolated the root of your problem, take action. If you lack self-respect and respect from others because of sin, confess it to God and claim His forgiveness (1 John 1:9). Begin now to conform your lifestyle to that of Jesus Christ, to more and more conform to His image (see 2 Cor. 3:18).

If your negative inner feelings are based only on *your* view of yourself without valid reasons, share these innermost anxieties with someone you really trust, someone who will accept you, listen to you, not pronounce more judgment upon you.

Note: This is what Christian husbands who really love as Christ loves should be able to do. But be careful, you may threaten your husband because he may blame himself for your inner feelings. If he becomes defensive and doesn't listen, he'll accentuate your problem and make you feel more unworthy and even more guilty.

Suggestion: You might have him read this chapter and particularly this paragraph and it may help him to understand what you're feeling.

Tell him first that you feel your problem is one of inferiority and related to an improper self-image. Tell him your need for an understanding and sympathetic listener—one to whom you can pour out all of your feelings of anxiety and stress, even your feelings of resentment that may stem from the fact that he has not been a good listener.

However, if you feel your husband cannot handle your problem, seek another trusted friend, preferably a mature Christian woman, and share your problem. Realize, however, that if your problem is too deep and difficult, you may need to talk to your pastor or another competent Christian counselor.

Step D: *If your problem is basically spiritual,* here are some Scriptures for you to memorize that will help you overcome sin in your life:

• "Thy word I have treasured in my heart, that I may not sin against Thee" (Ps. 119:11, *NASB*).

• "Therefore, I urge you, brothers, in view of God's mercy, to offer your bodies as living sacrifices, holy and pleasing to God—which is your spiritual worship. Do not conform any longer to the pattern of this world, but be transformed by the renewing of your mind. Then you will be able to test and approve what God's will is—his good, pleasing and perfect will" (Rom. 12:1,2).

• "And if the Spirit of him who raised Jesus from the dead is living in you, he who raised Christ from the dead will also give life to your mortal bodies through his Spirit, who lives in you" (Rom. 8:11).

• "No temptation has seized you except what is common to man. And God is faithful; he will not let you be tempted beyond what you can bear. But when you are tempted, he

will also provide a way out so that you can stand up under it" (1 Cor. 10:13).
• "I can do everything through him who gives me strength" (Phil. 4:13).
• "If we confess our sins, he is faithful and just and will forgive us our sins and purify us from all unrighteousness" (1 John 1:9).

If your problem is basically psychological, here are some Scriptures that will help you to build your self-image:
• "For Thou didst form my inward parts; Thou didst weave me in my mother's womb. I will give thanks to Thee, for I am fearfully and wonderfully made; Wonderful are Thy works" (Ps. 139:13,14, *NASB*).
• "For I am convinced that neither death nor life, neither angels nor demons, neither the present nor the future, nor any powers, neither height nor depth, nor anything else in all creation, will be able to separate us from the love of God that is in Christ Jesus our Lord" (Rom. 8:38,39).
• "Therefore we do not lose heart. Though outwardly we are wasting away, yet inwardly we are being renewed day by day" (2 Cor. 4:16).
• "What is man that you are mindful of him, or the son of man that you care for him? You made him a little lower than the angels; you crowned him with glory and honor and put everything under his feet" (Heb. 2:6-8).

Footnotes

1. An elder in the New Testament church was to serve as a "pastor" or shepherd (Acts 20:28; 1 Pet. 5:1,2), a teacher (1 Tim. 3:2; Titus 1:9), and a manager of the flock of God (1 Tim. 3:4,5; 5:17). Interestingly, a deacon's function is never spelled out; the word itself means to be a servant and the role seems to be clearly illustrated in Acts 6:1-7. An elder's responsibility is delineated as being primarily responsible for the spiritual welfare of the church, whereas a deacon's role seems to be more culturally conditioned and related to the physical needs of God's people.

2. Hereafter, all italicized words and phrases in Scripture quotations are the author's and are added to emphasize certain concepts and ideas.

3. Charles B. Williams, *The New Testament in the Language of the People* (Chicago: Moody Press, 1972).

3 BE NOT
MALICIOUS
TALKERS

"In the same way, their wives are . . . [to be] not malicious talkers." (1 Tim. 3:11)

One of the most recurring problems for all of us is to be able to properly control our tongues. Although it is definitely difficult for both men and women (see 2 Tim. 3:3), Paul specifically focuses on this subject as it relates to women. Twice in his pastoral epistles, once when he wrote to Timothy and once when he wrote to Titus, he instructed these men to be on guard against this problem in the church. To Timothy he wrote that women who serve as models of Christian maturity must be "worthy of respect, *not malicious talkers*" (1 Tim. 3:11). And to Titus, he wrote, "Teach the older women to be reverent in the way they live, *not be slanderers* [or malicious talkers or gossips]" (Titus 2:3).

James (Jas. 3–4) speaks more specifically and dramatically about the tongue and its potential for evil than does any other New Testament writer.

The Measure of Maturity

"We all stumble in many ways," wrote James. But, "if anyone is never at fault in what he says, he is a perfect [or mature] man, able to keep his whole body in check" (Jas. 3:2).

No person ever reaches perfection in this life, that is in the absolute sense and meaning of the word. But James's point is crystal clear. How we use our tongues serves as a precise measurement of our Christian maturity. And if we can control our tongues, we can usually control every other part of our personality.

James uses three graphic illustrations to make his point. We can control a horse (a large animal) by placing a *tiny bit* in his mouth. And we can direct the course of a *large ship* in all kinds of weather with a very *small rudder.* And we can set a *whole forest* on fire with a *little spark* (see Jas. 3:3-5).

Again, James's point is obvious. The tongue is small, one of the smallest members of the body. But it is powerful. And the tongue is like a "fire." It is "a world of evil among the parts of the body," and it "corrupts the whole person." Just as a small spark can set a whole forest on fire, so the tongue can set "the whole course" of a person's "life on fire" (Jas. 3:5,6).

Put another way, how we use our tongues reflects on everything we do and affects everything we do, and every person we come in contact with. As a fire spreads through a forest, igniting everything in its path, so a rumor, a bit of gossip, or an accusation, spreads quickly and out of control. And every tongue that repeats the rumor adds more fuel to what soon can become a raging fire.

In describing the evil nature of the tongue, James becomes very specific. The source of all this wickedness, wrote James, is "hell" itself (Jas. 3:6). Satan is at the root of all gossip, malicious talk, and slander.

Interestingly, the very word Paul used to describe malicious talk, gossip and slandering in 1 Timothy and Titus is in essence the very word used for "Satan" or "devil" in the New Testament. The correlation, of course, is clear. Satan has been a slanderer and false accuser ever since he fell from his place of glory and honor in heaven. "There is no truth in him," said Jesus. He "is a *liar* and the *father of lies*" (John 8:44).

Satan is the root of *all evil*. And since the tongue is capable of *great evil*, the source of that evil is Satan himself, with enormous power over mankind. Thus James added: "All kinds of animals, birds, reptiles and creatures of the sea are tamed and have been tamed by man, but no man can tame the tongue. It is a restless evil, full of deadly poison" (Jas. 3:7,8).

The Solution: Godly Wisdom

According to James, there is no effective way to control the tongue of a person who desires to live for himself and Satan. But as Christians, we do have a source to help us control our tongues and we also have a responsibility to help each other mature in this area of our lives.

Following his discussion on the tongue and its potential for evil, James wrote about two kinds of wisdom: wisdom that "does not come down from heaven" and wisdom that "does." That which is not from heaven is "earthly, unspiritual, of the devil." And it reflects itself through "envy," "selfish ambition," "disorder," and "every evil practice" (Jas. 3:15,16).

By contrast, godly wisdom, which comes from heaven, is "first of all, pure; then peace-loving, considerate, submissive, full of mercy and good fruit, impartial and sincere." It raises a "harvest of righteousness" rather than starting a forest fire (Jas. 3:17,18).

True, man by himself cannot tame the tongue. He

needs a greater source than himself, and God is that source. To tap that source, James gives a two-pronged strategy: First, he said, "submit yourselves . . . to God"; second, "resist the devil" (Jas. 4:7). Both are necessary. We must have both an offensive and defensive approach in living for Jesus Christ. On the one hand, we must "come near to God." We must seek His will; we must read His Word; and we must obey His commandments. On the other hand, we must resist Satan. We must not give in to his temptations to gossip, to slander, to speak evil of anyone. And if we follow this two-pronged strategy, James shares with us a wonderful promise. If we "come near to God . . . he will come near" to us (Jas. 4:8). And if we "resist the devil . . . he will flee" from us (Jas. 4:7).

The diagram on page 31 will help to put these truths in perspective.

Three Categories of Gossip

There are at least three kinds of gossip among Christians in the twentieth century.

The first kind of gossip is malicious gossip. This is what James is talking about. Malicious gossip is consciously and deliberately hurtful. It is based in envy and rooted in flagrant selfishness. It is designed to break up relationships and destroy friendships. And it can manifest itself in all kinds of evil deeds.

The second kind of gossip is rationalization. It is far more subtle than malicious gossip. What makes rationalization so dangerous is that it often results from self-deception. Rooted and based in the same motives as malicious gossip, the person who rationalizes has convinced herself (himself) that she is doing it for "the good" of the other person. She may disguise it as "prayer interest" and "personal concern." Nevertheless rationalization is very destructive.

The third kind of gossip is "innocent" gossip. This involves a person who truly is concerned, but who is, to a certain extent, unwise and insensitive to other people's feelings. Innocent gossip is sometimes motivated by a desire to be "helpful," but in reality, the gossiper may be trying to prove to others "how helpful she really is." In

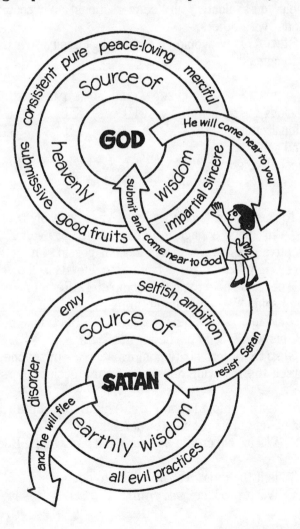

this situation there is a very fine line between "selfish" and "unselfish" motives. All Christians must beware of this kind of gossip.

A Personal or Group Project

The following questions and suggestions are designed to help you evaluate your "conversations" and "communications" with others.

Step A: How would you generally classify your use of the tongue:

	NEVER	LITTLE	SOMETIMES	FREQUENTLY
Malicious gossip	☐	☐	☐	☐
Rationalization and self-deceptive gossip	☐	☐	☐	☐
Innocent gossip	☐	☐	☐	☐

To check your "maturity level," it is probably true that most Christians engage in both "a little" or "some" self-deceptive gossip as well as innocent gossip. The goal, of course, is to eliminate it from your life-style; however, you'll never be able to do this completely. Remember what James said: "We all stumble in many ways. If anyone is *never* at fault in what he says, he is a perfect man, able to keep his whole body in check" (Jas. 3:2).

Step B: Before sharing information about anyone, ask yourself the following questions from a positive perspective:

1. Is this information *pure?* Will it contribute to the building up of this person (or persons)?

2. Will it help create *harmony* and *peace* in the Body of Christ?

3. Is it the most *merciful* thing to do?

4. Will it produce *good fruit?*

5. Does it reflect a *submissive* attitude on my part?

6. Am I truly *sincere* and *unselfish* in wanting to share this information?

7. Am I being *impartial* and *objective*? Do I really have the facts?

8. Am I truly being *considerate* of this person in sharing this information?

Now ask yourself these questions *from a negative perspective*:

1. Do I feel any *envy* towards this person? Do I want to hurt someone?

2. Am I motivated by *selfish ambitions*?

3. Will this create *disorder* and *lack of unity* in the Body of Christ?

4. Am I practicing *evil* or *good*?

Step C: If there is reason for communicating negative information about another Christian to someone else in the Body of Christ, then consider the following biblical injunctions and procedure:

• "If your brother sins against you, go and show him his fault, just between the two of you. If he listens to you, you have won your brother over. But if he will not listen, take one or two others along, so that 'every matter may be established by the testimony of two or three witnesses.' If he refuses to listen to them, tell it to the church; and if he refuses to listen even to the church, treat him as you would a pagan or a tax collector" (Matt. 18:15-17).

• "Do not rebuke an older man harshly, but exhort him as if he were your father. Treat younger men as brothers, older women as mothers, and younger women as sisters, with absolute purity" (1 Tim. 5:1,2).

Note: This instruction was given to Timothy by Paul. How does this apply to women who are in positions of leadership within the Body of Christ?

• "Do not entertain an accusation against an elder unless

it is brought by two or three witnesses. Those who sin are to be rebuked publicly, so that the others may take warning" (1 Tim. 5:19).

Note: Again this was an instruction given to Timothy. How does this apply to women who are in leadership roles?

Step D: Consider the following Scripture verses for meditation, memorization and guidance in using the tongue:

• "Death and life are in the power of the tongue, and those who love it will eat its fruit" (Prov. 18:21, *NASB*).

• "He who guards his mouth and his tongue guards his soul from troubles" (Prov. 21:23, *NASB*).

• "Like apples of gold in settings of silver is a word spoken in right circumstances" (Prov. 25:11, *NASB*).

• "Like a club and a sword and a sharp arrow is a man who bears false witness against his neighbor" (Prov. 25:18, *NASB*).

4 TO BE
TEMPERATE

"In the same way, their wives are to be . . . temperate."
(1 Tim. 3:11)

In this particular instance, Paul was no doubt cautioning Timothy against appointing a woman to any kind of leadership role in the church who is not self-controlled—particularly in the area of drinking wine. Many first-century women who were converted out of paganism (and that was the norm) were just as much involved in worldly practices as men.

First-Century Intemperance
Drunkenness was not uncommon. In fact, in those days many women probably used wine as a means to alleviate the emotional pain of having to fulfill the role expected of a woman. Who wouldn't want to "forget" the problems of just being a "slave," a "convenience," a "bearer of children in order to enhance a man's reputation in the community." Women who had no hope beyond this

life would be especially susceptible to drinking. And they had no hope. As Paul said to the Ephesians, "Remember that at that time you were separate from Christ, excluded from citizenship in Israel and foreigners to the covenants of the promise, *without hope* and *without God* in the world" (Eph. 2:12).

But Jesus Christ changed all that. Knowing the Saviour gives all people—*both* men and women—eternal hope. And furthermore, He gives women a new goal in *this* life. Spiritually, she is in a position of equality with men. For as Paul wrote to the Galatians, "There is neither Jew nor Greek, slave nor free, *male nor female* . . . in Christ Jesus," we "are all *one*" (Gal. 3:28). And Peter exhorted men to treat their wives as "heirs," heirs of "the gracious gift of life" (1 Pet. 3:7).

Paul, of course, put it very straight and heavy when he told men they were to love their wives "just as Christ loved the church" (Eph. 5:25). This meant no more physical and psychological abuse! No more playing around! No more taking her for granted! In Christ there was to be a brand new relationship. And this, of course, changed a woman's whole environment, and in changing her environment, it changed her life.

But old habits are difficult to break. Emotional and psychological hurt doesn't disappear overnight. It took time for some of these New Testament women to develop Christian maturity in all aspects of their lives. And lack of control in the area of drinking wine was a persistent temptation, especially since partaking of wine was a common custom of the day, even among Christians. Knowing when to stop was a constant problem, and still is for some to this day.

But lack of control and temperance is a mark of spiritual immaturity. A woman who had this problem certainly could not be a spiritual leader and an example to other

Christians. Furthermore, she would be a very poor witness to the pagan community.

Paul developed the same sequence of maturity traits in his letter to Titus when he admonished the older women to be examples to younger women. "Teach the older women," he wrote, "to be reverent in the way they live [worthy of respect], not to be slanderers [not malicious talkers] or *addicted to much wine* [to be temperate]" (Titus 2:3).

Twentieth-Century Intemperance

There is, of course, a literal application of Paul's statement to twentieth-century women, even in the sophisticated American culture. And with our "so-called" sophistication in values has come a "sophistication" in indulgence. The variety of addictive-type beverages has multiplied, and have been made "delightfully attractive" by multi-color advertisements in magazines, on billboards and over television. And, of course, "before" and "after" dinner drinks have become the norm in our "eat-out" society.

You might also think psychological and emotional stress has diminished in a culture where we have so many opportunities and technological advantages. Not so! There seem to be as many frustrated women today as ever before, even in a society where they are supposed to be treated as "human beings." There are increased pressures, new demands and unbelievable "performance standards" in the American culture. Consequently, there are multitudes of women who are seeking escape from their problems through alcohol.

But with sophistication in culture comes not only increased frustration, but also more "escape routes." Now we have drugs (both acceptable and unacceptable kinds), tobacco that is packaged in various shapes and sizes, delicious and exotic food, beautiful clothing styles that change every season, clubs, golf courses—and many more. All can be taken in excess, as escape from reality. And, of course, certain behavior in some of us is a carry-over of habits we formed before we were converted to Jesus Christ.

There are many Christian women who would never take a drop of alcohol. However, they "over-eat" with every degree of regularity. Interestingly, the Bible condemns over-indulgence in both areas of life (see Prov. 23:19-21). What is most contradictory, of course, is the woman who *judges* another (which the Bible condemns) for drinking wine moderately (which the Bible does *not* condemn). Which one is sinning against God?

Don't misunderstand! I'm not advocating drinking wine even moderately, though we certainly could not forbid it on the basis of Scripture, except when it becomes a mode of behavior that causes another Christian brother or sister to stumble and sin. If drinking wine hurts a fellow Christian, causing him to partake against his conscience (see Rom. 14:19-21; 1 Cor. 8:9-13; 10:31-33), then I must govern my life by a broader and higher principle—the principle of love (see Rom. 14:15-21; 1 Cor. 10:31).

But even here many Christians misinterpret the Scriptures. Some equate an "attitude of disagreement" with offense (see 1 Cor. 8:13, *KJV*). When one Christian disagrees with another Christian's freedom, it may not be a matter of offense. In fact, it could be judging—which the Bible condemns (see Rom. 14:3,4). However, when a Christian (with a "weak conscience") actually does what you do but sins in the process because he violates his own conscience, then you have offended him. You have caused him to stumble and to deteriorate even further in his Christian life.

What we are saying is that a Christian must be consistent. Temperance applies to many things in life, including "eating food." Temperance also applies to the way a woman spends money on herself, on her family, on her home. A woman must be temperate in all the means she uses to ease her frustration and stress and to satisfy her basic needs and desires. We can go to excess in almost everything we do. The Bible teaches temperance and self-control in all things (see 1 Cor. 10:23–11:1).

A Personal or Group Project

The following project is designed to help you evaluate your life-style in the area of "being temperate" and then to help you make the needed changes to conform to God's plan for your life.

Step A: Realize that there is an element of "relativity" in determining what is excessive. This varies with individuals. For example, some people have a greater source of income by which they can do a lot more things. Relatively speaking, they are not indulgent nor are they obsessed with things. They just have more of everything. And if they are mature Christians, they also have more to share and to give others. And if they are truly mature in Christ, they will be good stewards of God's good gifts.

Step B: Realize also that almost everything, in itself, is not wrong or evil. It is how these things are used and the degree to which they control us. For example, food is good and necessary, but when we are obsessed with eating to the point that it affects our spiritual, physical, and psychological well-being, we are sinning against ourselves and God.

Even drugs are one of God's greatest blessings to mankind. But when used as a permanent crutch, especially in the psychological realm, they can affect us negatively and diminish our usefulness for God.

Note: There are certain occasions when drugs are necessary throughout life in order to assist a person to live a balanced life (for example, as with epilepsy or with some stress syndromes that appear as a permanent part of the personality). But these are the exceptions, not the rule. Every Christian must beware of trying to solve problems superficially while ignoring the deeper causes.

Step C: The following questions will assist you in evaluating your own personal life-style:

1. Am I *controlled* by any habits that were part of my non-Christian life-style? Intemperance usually involves a lack of self-control—*over*-eating, *over*-spending, *over*-sleeping, *over*-working, or *over*-indulging in anything!

2. What are my *motives* for doing what I do? Some people overeat when they are under stress. Some people are chain-smokers because they are nervous. Some people overdrink because they are anxious. Some people overspend on clothes and items for the home because they feel inferior and insecure. Some people travel a great deal to run away from personal problems and basic responsibilities. Can *you* list other reasons why people are excessive in the things they do?

3. Are my problems *psychological* or purely *habitual*? There is a very fine line between these two causes. However, there is usually a distinction. A person who has psychological causes for intemperance operates at an obsessive level which doesn't really make sense to him. The very thought of change is threatening and causes even more anxiety.

The kind of behavior just described, of course, is also *habitual*. But a person who lacks self-control simply because of a bad habit usually doesn't find nearly the stress in trying to change her life-style. It may be painful and difficult, but it is far more easily solved.

Step D: If at this point you feel you actually have a problem with intemperance in some area of your life, the following suggestions will help you solve the problem:

1. Talk to several mature Christians whom you trust. Ask them to help you evaluate whether or not your concern is legitimate.

Warning: Some Christians have an oversensitive conscience. They have deep feelings of guilt about almost everything they do. They can never spend money on themselves without being obsessed with the knowledge that there are people in the world who have nothing to eat. People like this are *over*-sensitive. This kind of behavior usually develops because she was constantly reminded of these things when she was a small child. Some parents actually use this kind of tactic to get children to eat their food. Obviously it is not the way to develop a healthy personality.

2. If the people you talk to agree that you really have a serious problem, ask them to help you work out a plan for overcoming your difficulty and then to pray for you regularly.

3. If you continue to have difficulty controlling yourself—for example, in eating food—seek professional help, especially from a Christian psychiatrist. He will be able to deal with your problem from three perspectives—the physical, the psychological and the spiritual. The problem *could* be rooted in one or all of these areas.

Warning: This kind of problem is not easily solved. There is no magic formula. So don't get discouraged. Determine that with God's help you can "kick the habit."

The following realistic case studies may help you and others:

Woman A is a person who cannot stop spending money. When she is in a drug store, she buys perfume, spray deodorant, toothpaste—even when she doesn't need it. Her bathroom is full of half-used containers, to which she continues to add. When she is in a clothing store, she has an insatiable desire to buy a new dress. Her closet is full of dresses she has worn only one time. What plan would you suggest to this woman to help her overcome her intemperance in these areas?

Woman B is a compulsive eater. This may sound strange to you, but she actually overeats until she regurgitates so she can eat some more. Interestingly, she is not overweight and is a very attractive person. She loves Christ and is terribly disturbed by her problem. What do you think is this woman's problem? What would you recommend that she do?

Woman C has a problem with alcohol. She finds that in order to be a good sexual partner to her husband she has to overcome her inhibitions by drinking to the point where she is slightly inebriated. Otherwise, she cannot enjoy the experience. How would you counsel this woman?

Woman D wants to eat out all the time. She finds it difficult to cook meals, and she gets very bored around the house. Her husband complains because they never have enough money left to buy clothes and other things they need. Can you analyze this woman's problem? How would you help her?

Woman E is a chain-smoker. When she goes more than a couple of hours without a cigarette, she is "fit to be tied." She wants to quit, feels it's a bad example to her children and really is concerned that it's not a good example to her non-Christian friends. But she cannot seem to "kick" the habit. Any suggestions for this woman?

Woman F pops pills regularly. She began taking drugs to overcome severe headaches and back pains caused by a bad fall. Now she is dependent on drugs, even though her physical problems no longer exist. How does a problem like this evolve, and what should she do about it?

Warning: Simple Bible reading and prayer formulas usually do not help people like those just described. Furthermore, pronouncing judgment on them sometimes makes their problems worse. How would you, under these circumstances, relate the Word of God and prayer to their problem?

5 TO BE
TRUSTWORTHY
IN EVERYTHING

"In the same way, their wives are to be . . . trustworthy in everything." (1 Tim. 3:11)

I guess maybe I'm fortunate! Over the years, while serving in various Christian positions, I've had several superb secretaries—Girl Fridays, if you will—who have faithfully served at my side, helping me to carry out my various and sundry responsibilities. Without them it would have been virtually impossible to function effectively in the vocational positions in which I found myself. Without exception, and I consider it a tribute, I would evaluate every one of these girls as "trustworthy in everything."

Now, of course, they were no more *perfect* than I was or I am. Sure, they made mistakes. So did I! But as everyone knows who has served in an administrative role, a trustworthy secretary minimizes her boss' mistakes and, thank the Lord, often makes him "look good" when sometimes he should "look bad."

Of course, I must hasten to add that my greatest Girl Friday has been my wife. Her constant faithfulness as a wife and mother has been a consistent source of encouragement and motivation. Solomon, you were right! "He who finds a wife finds a good thing" (Prov. 18:22, *NASB*)—especially when she's "an excellent wife . . . . For her worth is far above jewels. The heart of her husband *trusts in her,* and he will have no lack of gain" (Prov. 31:10,11, *NASB*).

Paul, while stating the characteristics for the maturity level of a Christian woman, included the quality of "faithfulness" or "trustworthiness." And, said he, she should be trustworthy in *everything.*

Technically, this refers to a person who can be trusted to faithfully "transact business," to faithfully "carry out instruction" and to faithfully "discharge official duties." One of the most secure feelings I have is when I have to be away from my office—especially when I'm out of town—and can be assured that the work will be carried out properly, that proper explanations will be given for my absence and that communication is adequate to everyone concerned.

Some Biblical Examples

There are numerous women in the Bible who could certainly be cited as being trustworthy Christians. In fact, Paul mentioned at least five in his closing greetings to the Roman Christians. He described Priscilla (along with her husband Aquila) as being a fellow-worker in Christ and one who risked her very life for him (see Rom. 16:3). He also mentioned Mary, Tryphena and Tryphosa, and then Persis—all described as women who worked hard in the service of Jesus Christ (see Rom. 16:6,12). Others he mentioned were Lydia, Paul's first convert in Philippi (see Acts 16:14), and Timothy's mother, Eunice, whom Paul commended for her *faith,* and *faithfulness,* in nurturing Timothy in the holy Scriptures (see 2 Tim. 1:5; 3:14,15).

But the most specific New Testament examples of trustworthy Christians were several men who *faithfully* served with Paul in the ministry.

Tychicus is mentioned several times in the New Testament, especially in Paul's letter to the Ephesians and the Colossians. Paul commends him for his ability to *communicate clearly, accurately and fully*. To the Ephesians he wrote: "Tychicus, the dear brother and *faithful* [trustworthy] servant in the Lord, will *tell you everything*, so that you also may know how I am and what I am doing. I am sending him to you for this very purpose, *that you may know how we are*, and that he may encourage you" (Eph. 6:21,22).

To the Colossians, Paul said, "Tychicus will tell you *all the news* about me. He is a dear brother, a *faithful* [trustworthy] minister and fellow servant in the Lord. I am sending him to you *for the express purpose that you may know about our circumstances* and that he may encourage your hearts" (Col. 4:7-9).

It seems obvious that Paul aligned this man's ability to communicate adequately with the fact that he was *faithful* and *trustworthy*. And, of course, this makes sense, for no doubt, 90 percent of your trust in other people is based upon their ability to tactfully and accurately represent your point of view.

Epaphras is mentioned by Paul twice in his Colossian letter. Interestingly, the first references involved this "faithful minister" and his *communication*. First, this man initially *proclaimed* the gospel to the Colossians. Secondly, he was *the primary source* through whom Paul learned so much about the Colossians' spiritual development (Col. 1:7,8). When Paul closed the letter, he paid tribute to Epaphras' *faithfulness* to them: "Epaphras, who is one of you and a servant of Christ Jesus, sends greetings. He is always wrestling in prayer for you, that you may stand firm in all the will of God, mature and fully assured. I vouch for him that he is working hard for you and for those in Laodicea and Hierapolis" (Col. 4:12,13).

Onesimus is someone we know more about than we do Tychicus and Epaphras. It is very significant that Paul would use the word "faithful" or "trustworthy" (Col. 4:9) to describe this young man. In fact, Onesimus traveled with Tychicus to help him communicate Paul's circumstances to the Colossians. "They will," wrote Paul speaking of both of them, "tell you everything that is happening here" (Col. 4:9).

Onesimus was a former slave, a very *untrustworthy* and useless young man, who ran away from Philemon's household (Philem. 11). He had no doubt stolen some of Philemon's possessions (v. 18) and for some unknown reason (other than God's sovereign involvement in his life), ended up in a Roman prison cell. Of all people, the man who was next to him was the apostle Paul, the man who had led his master to Christ (v. 19) and now was one of Philemon's best friends (vv. 7,22). Imagine the shock and surprise on Onesimus' face as it dawned on him who was sitting next to him!

To make a rather involved story short and simple, Paul also led Onesimus to Christ, nurtured him in the faith and eventually sent him back to Philemon, no longer as a useless slave but as a trustworthy brother in Christ. Eventually, this conniving, no-good and "untrustworthy" slave boy became one of Paul's most faithful and trustworthy traveling companions in preaching the gospel of Jesus Christ (see Col. 4:9).

Being "faithful" and "trustworthy," then, is a quality in life that demonstrates Christian maturity in both men and women; maturity that particularly enables the person to pass on information without omitting important details, without misrepresenting and without creating confusion.

But Paul's primary focus in 1 Timothy 3 is women—being mature women who are "trustworthy in everything." And to say the least, that is a rather all-inclusive qualification.

A Personal or Group Project

The following section includes several checklists for women involved in various twentieth-century roles. This section is designed to help you discover whether or not you are "trustworthy in everything." The lists are also "starters"—suggestions to get you thinking.

1. For Christian wives and mothers:
☐ I can be trusted to prepare meals adequately and on time.
☐ I can be trusted to keep the house neat and clean.
☐ I can be trusted to keep clothes washed and in order.
☐ I can be trusted to do the shopping regularly and in an orderly way, planning ahead and taking advantage of "specials."
☐ I can be trusted to keep confidential information truly confidential.
☐ I can be trusted to always remain loyal and true to my husband spiritually, morally and in every other way.
☐ I can be trusted to spend money carefully—watching for special sales, planning ahead and buying cautiously.

Note: Don't be deceived at this juncture. Inexpensive purchases are not always good buys and do not always represent good stewardship. It sometimes pays to spend more for quality merchandise that will, in the long run, be a better investment.

A Special Assignment: Compare the above checklist with the description of an excellent wife in Proverbs 31:10-31. What additional questions could you add to this checklist?

2. For Christian secretaries, administrative assist-

ants, and other "Girl Friday" roles:

☐ I am always discreet.

☐ I keep my desk well-ordered and my office neat and clean.

☐ I keep my superior's desk in good order, regularly organizing his working materials, notes and correspondence.

☐ I keep his (or her) office furniture dusted and in good order.

☐ I keep him (or her) constantly abreast of all communiqués.

☐ I make notes of all important instructions and report back when all items are cared for.

☐ I handle all incoming calls courteously and tactfully.

☐ I welcome visitors, making them feel at home.

☐ When it is impossible for callers to get through or visitors to see my supervisor, I tactfully communicate "why."

☐ I always follow through on instructions, giving careful attention to details.

☐ I proofread all correspondence carefully, never sending out letters that are carelessly done.

☐ I handle all information confidentially.

☐ I do all I can to compensate for my superior's weaknesses.

☐ I do all I can to facilitate his (or her) work.

☐ I can be trusted to correctly represent his (or her) viewpoint in all communication.

Note: Some women work for individuals who are inefficient and insensitive. In these cases, do all you can to help your superior become more efficient. If the problem is unbearable, you'll need to communicate directly, but sensitively and with love.

3. For Christian women in other vocations:

☐ I always follow through on instructions.

☐ I do my work cheerfully.

☐ I do my work conscientiously and carefully.

☐ I communicate adequately to everyone concerned.

☐ I am always honest, ethical and a person of integrity.

☐ I am tactful and sensitive in my working relationships with other employees.

☐ I do all I can to properly interpret my superiors to others.

☐ I defend my superiors—but without being dishonest.

☐ I am cautious how I mix my Christian witness with my business—never taking company time to talk about spiritual issues (unless prompted to do so by a superior).

☐ I am always teachable.

Suggestion: Read Christ's story of the talents in Matthew 25:14-30. What guidelines can you gain from this story that will help to be a *faithful* servant of others?

Several Steps to Improve Your Trustworthiness

If you have lost credibility because of carelessness, either in marriage or on the job, openly acknowledge your mistakes and indicate your desire to improve yourself. Never hesitate to ask for a second chance. But be super cautious! Don't drop the ball the second time.

Note: Credibility, once lost, can be rebuilt. But it takes double effort. Don't be discouraged. And above all, don't defend yourself when you're wrong.

If you are misinterpreted, or constantly fail because of poor communication between you and your husband or you and your superior, you must communicate this problem clearly yourself. But be sure to do so carefully, tactfully and as non-threateningly as possible.

Note: Seek advice from several mature Christian friends before making your move. And pray much about it.

Don't blame others for your mistakes. If you do, you

lose credibility very quickly.

Don't lose your temper. It is better to say nothing than to say it "emotionally."

Ask for suggestions to improve your trustworthiness. Don't be afraid to ask for feedback. Though this may be initially threatening, in the end it will provide you with greater security.

Note: What additional suggestions can you make to help others trust you more?

A Final Challenge

Remember that God the Father and Jesus Christ the Lord serve as our supreme examples in being trustworthy and faithful in all things. Note the following verses:

• "No temptation has seized you except what is common to man. And God *is faithful;* he will not let you be tempted beyond what you can bear. But when you are tempted, he will also provide a way out so that you can stand up under it" (1 Cor. 10:13).

• "May God himself, the God of peace, sanctify you through and through. May your whole spirit, soul and body be kept blameless at the coming of our Lord Jesus Christ. The one who calls you is *faithful* and he will do it" (1 Thess. 5:23,24).

• "But the Lord is *faithful,* and he will strengthen and protect you from the evil one" (2 Thess. 3:3).

• "If we are faithless, he will remain *faithful,* for he cannot disown himself" (2 Tim. 2:13).

• "Let us hold unswervingly to the hope we profess, for he who promised is *faithful*" (Heb. 10:23).

• "If we confess our sins, *he is faithful* and just and will forgive us our sins and purify us from all unrighteousness" (1 John 1:9).

6 TO TEACH **WHAT** IS GOOD

"Likewise, teach the older women to be reverent in the way they live, not to be slanderers, or addicted to much wine, but to teach what is good. Then, they can train the younger women." (Titus 2:3,4)

These are the words of Paul to Titus, who like Timothy, was one of Paul's faithful traveling companions and fellow missionaries. After planting a church on the island of Crete, Paul asked Titus to remain for a time in order to help establish this young and growing family of believers. Later Paul wrote Titus a letter, giving him more specific instructions regarding how to *order* the life of the Cretan church.

Interestingly, much of what Paul had to say to Titus related directly to how individual Christians were to *order* their lives. And among the various groups that were mentioned in his letter, Paul included "older women." "Teach the *older women*," he said, and in turn, "they can train *the younger women*" (Titus 2:3,4).

There is no way to specifically categorize what Paul

meant by "older" and "younger" women any more than we can set a specific age level for men who serve as elders. One thing is clear however. Paul had two general categories in mind in this passage—those women who were "older" and those who were "younger," and these two categories are *always* in that chronological order. Though specific age levels vary, those who are "older" always bear the responsibility for setting a positive example for the "younger."

For example, in our present culture, high school girls are older than junior high girls so they are responsible to model Christianity for their younger sisters in Jesus Christ. The same is true of college age women and their relationship to high school girls. And so we move up and down the age scale—with older women always in a position of greater responsibility to demonstrate a consistent Christian life-style. Here, then, is a biblical principle that is supracultural, one that is always relevant at any time in history and in any specific geographical location and with any particular age group.

Note the correlation between Paul's instructions to Timothy (developed in the previous four chapters) and his instructions to Titus. In both letters, the first three qualifications for women, though stated differently, were in essence the same:

TO TIMOTHY Women are to be:	TO TITUS Women are:
worthy of respect	reverent in the way they live
not malicious talkers	not to be slanderers
temperate	not addicted to wine

It is with the fourth qualification in both letters that we see a different thrust. To Timothy, he wrote that women were to be "trustworthy in everything"—the subject in our last chapter. To Titus, he said that they were "to teach what is good"—the subject of this present chapter.

Effective Teaching

How can we effectively communicate to others what is involved in a Christian life-style? Obviously, this process includes both teaching by example and by direct instruction. But Paul made it clear throughout his writings (his direct instruction) that foundational to his instructions was his own Christian example. This was why he could write to the Corinthians, "Follow my *example,* as I follow the *example* of Christ" (1 Cor. 11:1). And why he could also remind the Thessalonians, "You are witnesses, and so is God, of how holy, righteous and blameless we were among you who believed" (1 Thess. 2:10).

In his letter to Titus, Paul zeros in on this same basic concept. To "teach what is good" means, first of all *demonstrating* "goodness" with a Christian life-style. Thus he wrote "Teach the older women to be reverent in the *way they live,* not to be slanderers or addicted to wine, but (by contrast) to *teach what is good."*

Paul's next paragraph which was directed specifically at Titus' involvement in the teaching-learning process, made the point even clearer: "In everything set them an *example* by *doing* what is *good.* In your *teaching* show integrity, seriousness and soundness of speech that cannot be condemned, so that those who oppose you may be ashamed because they have nothing bad to say about us."

In other words, demonstrate with your life what you are trying to communicate. If you don't, what you are saying will be thrown right back in your face (Titus 2:7,8).

Paul's approach to teaching was show-and-tell. And "showing" was always foundational to "telling." But don't misunderstand! This does not mean the two cannot occur simultaneously. In some respects, the two are so intricately interwoven in the teaching-learning process that they cannot be separated. Even in "telling," *what* is said becomes meaningful by the *way* it is said—the attitude involved, the tone of voice, the very life-style that at that moment emerges and serves as a "loudspeaker," an amplification system, if you will, that truly helps people *hear* what we are saying.

But it is also true that what gives real weight and validity to verbal teaching is a consistent life-style and Christian example—what people see over the long haul. As people come to know you, as they observe your consistency, as they *see* your persistent love for Christ and others, your "words" take on more and more significance.

Effective Living

The English translations of the phrase "teaching what is good" (as well as similar ones) actually come from a single word in the Greek New Testament—*kalodidaskalos*. This particular injunction appears only once—in Titus 2:3. A *didaskalos* is a teacher, and *kalos* is often translated "good." Thus Paul literally is instructing older women to be "*teachers* of what is *good.*" Of course, the words "teacher" and "good" are used separately numerous times in the New Testament.

The word *kalos* also has various meanings in the New Testament in addition to "good." The Greeks often used the word to refer to anything that was beautiful in form, excellence, goodness or usefulness. But when Paul used the word with the concept of "teaching," it is quite clear from the context what he had in mind. "In everything set them an example by *doing* what is *good.*" Then he added, "In your *teaching* show integrity, seriousness and soundness of speech." The correlation between "teaching" and "doing what is good" is abundantly clear. But let's look at a couple more examples.

Paul's Exhortation to Timothy

In Paul's first letter to Timothy, he dealt with numerous issues and problems. He warned against men who were teaching false doctrine and devoting "themselves to myths and endless genealogies" (1 Tim. 1:3,4). He also gave specific instructions regarding women, warning them not to put themselves in a position of authority over men (see 1 Tim. 2:12). He then very thoroughly specified the qualifications for leaders in the church, including women leaders (see 1 Tim. 3:1-13). And then he cautioned against following false *teachings* regarding marriage and the use of food (see 1 Tim. 4:1-5).

Following these instructions to Timothy, who in turn was to pass them on to the Christians in Ephesus, Paul made several statements that are directly related to the subject of this lesson, "teaching what is good." "If you point *these things* out to the brothers," he wrote, "you will be a *good* minister of Christ Jesus, brought up in the *truths* of faith and of the *good* teaching that you have followed. Have nothing to do with *godless myths* and *old wives tales*" (1 Tim. 4:6,7).

Paul's point is clear. To "teach what is *good*," to be a "*good* minister," to be involved in "*good* teaching" means communicating what is true, what is from God, what is God's will and way. In short, it means teaching the Word of God—not false doctrine that is based on "myths and old wives' tales."

So, the mark of Christian maturity for a Christian woman is to know God's Word, to know what is really sound doctrine. It's only as you know what God says that you can "teach what is good." For that which is *good* is from God.

Before we leave this passage we must note one other very important correlation. To be a "*good* minister of Christ Jesus," to be involved in "*good* teaching," Timothy had to "train [himself] to be godly" (1 Tim. 4:7).

And then to make the point very clear, Paul reiterated with elaboration, "Command and *teach* these things. Don't let anyone look down on you because you are young, but set an *example* for the believers in speech, in life, in love, in faith and in purity" (2 Tim. 4:11,12).

Again, the correlation is obvious. Effective teaching must be based on a proper example, a dynamic life-style that illustrates Christian doctrine. Thus Paul concluded this emphasis with a dynamic exhortation to Timothy, "Watch your *life* and *doctrine* closely" (2 Tim. 4:16).

One thing more from this passage! Timothy was young, how young we're not really sure. But obviously he was younger than many he was teaching. Just so, in many churches today many Christian women in leadership roles are chronologically younger than the women they are leading and teaching. If you're in this category, draw strength from Paul's exhortation and Timothy's example. Let me repeat it: "Don't let anyone look down on you *because you are young,* but set an example for the believers in speech, in life, in love, in faith and in purity."

In other words, even though Paul directed the "older men" to teach the "younger," and gave them the primary responsibility, he also makes it clear with his letters to Timothy that in some instances, "younger women" have a similar responsibility to older women. The difference is that the younger women will have even a greater challenge to demonstrate with their lives their maturity in Christ in order to build a bridge for more direct teaching.

Paul's Exhortation to the Thessalonians

Paul in essence expressed the same concerns in his letter to the Christians at Thessalonica. And that concern was that they not be led astray by false teaching—teaching that was *not* good. Consequently, he wrote: "Do not put out the Spirit's fire; do not treat prophecies with contempt. Test everything. Hold on to the *good.* Avoid every kind of evil" (1 Thess. 5:19-22).

To understand what Paul was saying, we must remember that first-century Christians did not have the New Testament as we have it today. In fact, this letter to the Thessalonians may have been the first piece of inspired New Testament literature they had ever seen; and conceivably, this letter and the second one may have been the *only* inspired literature that some of these believers ever saw. Their source of teaching came directly from gifted individuals, particularly the apostles and the prophets, who were inspired by the Holy Spirit to speak forth God's truth.

But the problem they often faced was teaching from *false* prophets, the very thing Paul warned Timothy against. "Some will abandon the faith," he wrote, "and follow deceiving spirits and things taught by demons" (1 Tim. 4:1). And likewise, in Thessalonica some individuals were claiming to be prophesying by means of the Holy Spirit, whereas they were actually prompted by evil spirits—or their own "spirits." Thus Paul warned, "Do not quench the Spirit; do not despise prophetic utterances. But *examine everything carefully;* hold fast to that which is good" (1 Thess. 5:19-21, *NASB*).

In other words, Paul warned them to listen carefully to those who claimed to be prophets of God, speaking the truth of God. They were not to interfere with the Spirit of God. But he very quickly warned them to test carefully everything that was being said, to reject any doctrine that seemed to be false and evil, and to "hold on to the good."

At this point, you may wonder how anyone in the New Testament world could discern what was *good* and what was *evil.* Fortunately, God gave certain individuals special gifts to enable them to "distinguish between spirits" (1

Cor. 12:10). Evidently, those with the gift of discernment could very quickly detect false prophets. This is why it was doubly important that all members of the Body of Christ function. All were needed to maintain a proper direction doctrinally.

Today, God has already spoken. We have not only the Thessalonian letters, but many more in our New Testament—letters written to numerous churches all over the New Testament world. But Paul's warning is still applicable to Christians.

There are many "false prophets" who improperly interpret the Scriptures, making them teach things they do not. Think of the many false cults and isms that permeate the twentieth-century scene, promoting doctrines that are contrary to the Word of God.

A mature woman of God, then, knows her Bible— what it says, what it means. And most important, she has applied it to her life. She truly is in a position to *teach what is good.*

A Personal or Group Project

The following personal project is designed to help you as a Christian woman, become a person who can "teach what is good."

Step A: How much are you living out in your life what you already *know* about the Bible? Remember, Paul was concerned that we first of all teach by example. The following project will assist you in determining areas for improvement:

1. List the areas in your life where you feel you *are* putting into practice what you already know about *good* doctrine. For example, you may feel you are a good homemaker, that you are given to hospitality, that you are faithful to your husband, etc. What would *you* list about yourself?

2. List the areas in your life where you feel you are *not* putting into practice what you already know about *good* doctrine.

Suggestion: Get together with several women in a small group and brainstorm on areas where the average Christian woman has difficulty practicing what she really believes. This will help you get input from others who are having similar problems. And do remember, you're not alone. Most Christian women (and men) *do* have similar problems in putting into practice what they already know about good doctrine.

To help you with this process, following are some of the areas listed by the group of Christian women who first worked through this study on *The Measure of a Woman:*

☐ Having a forgiving spirit
☐ Being unselfish
☐ Controlling anger
☐ Overcoming worry
☐ Admitting mistakes
☐ Being consistent

What would you add to this list from your own experience?

3. Now that you have developed a list, beside each area of weakness, suggest ways to improve in that area. Be specific. For example, what can a Christian mother do to be more consistent with her children?

Following are some suggested solutions to generate ideas for you and/or your group:

☐ When having a problem with forgiveness, be open and honest with the person involved. Talk out the problem.
☐ Try to understand *why* you feel selfish. Talk to another mature Christian woman about the problem. Seek her advice; pray together.
☐ When having a problem with anger, make sure you are getting sufficient rest and diversion from your regular daily routine. Also, are you feeling guilty for anger that

is normal and natural? Remember, Paul said, "In your anger do not sin" (Eph. 4:26). There is anger that *is* sinful, and there is anger that is unavoidable. Are you differentiating the two? (For a more comprehensive treatment on this subject, see *The Measure of a Man*, chapter 11, entitled "Not Quick-Tempered.")

Note: One of the greatest places for an "older woman" to teach a "younger woman" is in the home—"mother to daughter."

Step B: How well do you know your Bible? Are you familiar with the basic doctrines of Christianity? Can you detect false doctrine when you are listening to a speaker, reading an article, or a book, talking to a friend? For example, can you explain and support from Scripture what it means to be "justified by faith"? What about your view of the Word of God? Can you defend our belief that it is inspired of God and free from error in the original? Can you explain the Trinity? What about the deity of Christ, His incarnation, His substitutionary death? What about the truths regarding His second coming? Do you understand the ministry of the Holy Spirit today—His regeneration, His indwelling, His sealing, His baptism?

What about the concept of man in the Scriptures? Can you explain the fall, sin, and how you can be saved from the penalty and power of sin?

Then there's the subject of sanctification, the assurance of salvation, and the security we have in Christ.

All of these are important subjects and doctrines in Scripture. To be able to "teach what is good," we must do all we can to have a sufficient grasp of these subjects. If you feel you have areas of weakness in your knowledge of Scripture, and most of us do, there's only one solution. You must be involved either in personal or group study of the Bible.

Note: Most Christians, men and women alike, lack the

specific skills and discipline to engage in personal Bible study on a consistent basis. Furthermore, even if we want to, there are so many demands and distractions in our culture that keep us from following through. It is at this point we need the mutual encouragement that comes from other members of the Body of Christ.

Suggestion: Join in a small group Bible study. Set up standards in the group. For example, expect everyone in the group to do personal study in preparation for the group study. This has been one of the factors that has contributed to the success of Bible Study Fellowship, an organization that fosters group and personal Bible study among women.

And here's another suggestion. If you want to get started on a personal study to increase your knowledge in some of the areas just mentioned, select a good book that deals with the basic doctrines of Scripture. For example, one that will give you a complete overview of the doctrines of Scripture is *Major Bible Themes* by John F. Walvoord and Lewis Sperry Chafer.[1]

A Final Challenge

Jesus Christ called Himself the *Good* Shepherd (see John 10:11,14), and indeed He is our supreme example of goodness. He is also our supreme example for *teaching what is good*. Remember Paul's words to the Corinthians? He said, "Follow my example, as I follow the example of Christ" (1 Cor. 11:1). This should be every Christian's goal—to be able with our life and words to invite people to *follow us* as we follow Christ and reflect *His* goodness.

Remember: We cannot teach what we do not know! How well do you really know Jesus Christ?

Footnote

1. John F. Walvoord & Lewis S. Chafer, *Major Bible Themes,* rev. ed. (Grand Rapids: Zondervan Publishing House, 1974).

7 TO LOVE THEIR
HUSBANDS

"Likewise, teach the older women . . . then they can train the younger women to love their husbands." (Titus 2:3,4)

Jane has been married for 15 years. She is a Christian and so is her husband, Jim. And she has tried to be a good Christian wife and still wants to be. But over the years she has, to use her own words, "fallen out of love" with Jim. Yes, she still respects him, submits to his authority (at least outwardly), but inside she doesn't feel attracted to him. In fact, she often finds herself resenting him. Though she hates to admit it, she's most happy when he's not around.

And sex? Well, she has been dutiful because the Bible says she should. Most of the time she endures the relationship, though at times she admits to some physical satisfaction. Emotionally, however, she feels no real "oneness" with Jim. She could really live without the "physical satisfaction" because the "emotional satisfaction" disappeared a long time ago. In fact, the "emotional resentments" are often so overpowering that she doesn't really enjoy the "physical satisfaction."

This case study, though fictitious, represents one of the most serious problems facing many Christian women in the twentieth century. Though various situations differ in their particulars, the general problem is often the same: "feelings" in the relationship are either missing or negative. To complicate the situation, there is often a great deal of guilt associated with the problem, making matters worse. This is particularly true among Christian women who take the Bible seriously and who really want to please God in all they do.

Since the Bible clearly teaches "wifely submission" and "responsibility," Christian women try hard to obey the Lord, even though they don't "feel like it." And when they don't respond as they believe they should, they are immediately covered over with guilt, which compounds the problem. Of course, some insensitive and/or threatened Christian husbands really know how to use "Bible verses" to their advantage, thereby creating more anxiety and guilt for their wives.

A First-Century Problem, Too

Evidently, this was also a problem in New Testament days, which we should be able to understand. Oftentimes wives were only used as "child-bearers" and, in many instances, not at all as "lovers." It was rather normative for men to have extramarital affairs in order to meet their physical and psychological needs. Their wives, however, became the means to produce legitimate offspring and heirs in the family.

In some respects, this arrangement probably took some of the pressure off of these wives in that they at least did not have to "perform" sexually on a regular basis. But on the other hand, it deprived them of needed physical intimacy with their husbands and created an environment where no real love existed—either on the "behavioral" or the "feeling" level.

Of course, wives had no real choice but to accept circumstances as they were. For there were few, if any, alternative life-styles that would meet their daily needs.

These moral, spiritual, and psychological problems were not automatically solved when one or both partners converted to Christ. They continued to exist and to plague many marriage relationships, as they do today. And in some instances, no doubt the problems became worse before they got better.

But because these problems existed, Paul had to deal with them. And he did, from two perspectives. First, he dealt with marriage relationships at the reciprocal and behavioral level. He exhorted Christian wives to change their attitudes and actions toward both their saved and unsaved husbands. They were to respect them, submit to them, and obey them (see Eph. 5:22; Col. 3:18). They were to develop an inner beauty of soul and spirit—the "unfading beauty of a gentle and quiet spirit, which" wrote Peter, "is of great worth in God's sight" (1 Pet. 3:4).

Paul also got down to the heart of the matter in his remarks to Christian husbands. He exhorted them to love their wives "just as Christ loved the church" (Eph. 5:25; Col. 3:19). Peter added another dimension, "Husbands, in the same way be considerate as you live with your wives, and treat them with respect as the weaker partner and as heirs with you of the gracious gift of life, so that nothing will hinder your prayers" (1 Pet. 3:7). Both Paul's and Peter's remarks represent the "bottom line" in solving many problems for a Christian wife. When a Christian husband loves his wife as Christ really loved the Church, normally his wife will respond at the behavioral as well as at the feeling level. But when he doesn't, frequently greater anxiety and resentment are created which almost invariably reflect themselves in negative behavior.

But this "formula," ideal as it is, does not always solve problems. It is basic, but not always the quick and easy solution. The formula is always foundational in helping a couple overcome their problems, but we must be prepared to go further. So consequently, Paul also dealt with the problem from another perspective, offering some additional suggestions for overcoming negative feelings. This, I believe, is Paul's focus when he exhorted Timothy to teach the older women to behave in a certain way in order that they might be able to "train younger women *to love their husbands.*"

In the phrase, "to *love* their husbands," the Greek word translated "love" is not the most common word for love in the New Testament. *Agapao* and *agape* are used most to refer to love that acts in a proper way, a love that does the right thing no matter what our feelings. Christ demonstrated this love most significantly when He went to the cross and suffered for mankind, even though, at the feeling level, His desire was to escape this pain and agony (see Matt. 26:38, 39). In spite of His painful ambivalence and His agony of soul, He asked that God's will be done. It is this kind of love a Christian man is to demonstrate towards his wife (see Eph. 5:25; Col. 3:19). It is this kind of love we are to have towards our neighbors, both Christians and non-Christians.

But the Greek word used by Paul in Titus 2:4 refers to a *phileo* love, often used to describe the "emotional" dimensions of love. *Phileo* involves "friendship." It expresses "delight" in doing something. It refers to doing something with "pleasure." This is why *agapao* is not used in the Bible to describe "sexual love," particularly sexual responsibility. "Sexual love" involves emotions and you cannot command a person to "feel" a certain way towards someone else. You *can* command a person to *do something* in spite of feelings. (Thus the Bible says, "Husbands, *love* your wives;" or more dramatically, it says, "*Love* your enemies.") But you cannot force a person to *feel positive* when he *feels negative*. Thus Paul worded the statement very carefully to Titus; older women were to "train the younger women to love their husbands."[1] The word "train" that Paul used here and the context in which he used it implies a process.[2] It was to be a process of learning, a process of coming to the place where wives felt "friendly" toward their husbands; where they felt "warm" and "secure" in their husbands' presence; where they had a deep sense of "trust" and "emotional commitment" toward them. And this, of course, would be a new experience for many first-century wives, for a number of marriages had never included this dimension before.

Paul made it very clear in this passage that this training process involved older women. They were to be "reverent in the way they lived"; they were "not to be slanderers or addicted to much wine"; rather, they were to "teach what is good." And "*then*," wrote Paul, they can *train* the younger women to "love their husbands." Putting it another way, these younger women needed a model, an example, a pattern. They needed to "see" and "experience" older women demonstrating loyalty, affection, and commitment to their own husbands. They needed to learn *how* to love.

A Personal or Group Project

Step A: At least two significant lessons emerge from a study of "biblical love" in the New Testament which we must put into practice to be mature Christians.

1. Actions take precedence over feelings. This is a difficult concept to implement in our behavior. It is difficult to do things we'd rather not do. But life is made up of these

demands. We must get up when we'd rather sleep. We must cook meals when we'd rather be watching television. We must wash clothes when we'd rather be playing tennis. And of course men have the same problem. They'd rather read the paper than play in the backyard with their sons— especially after a hard day's work. They'd rather kick off their socks and relax in the recliner than mow the lawn.

In many instances, positive feelings follow actions. This is normal. In fact, in many instances, positive feelings emerge *in the process* of doing what we know we must do. This is part of being human. And to be able to do so is a reflection of our maturity level.

Note: It is important to recognize that there are many instances in life when we'll not feel positive about doing something even for the person we respect and love the most. This again is normal. It should not be the cause of personal anxiety and guilt, unless we consistently "follow our feelings" rather than what we know to be right.

2. Feelings of affection can be learned. Many women in the New Testament who were converted to Christ had to learn for the first time what it means to "enjoy a relationship with their husbands." Affection *can* be learned. Paul certainly implied this in his statement in Titus. In most instances, affection is learned through *example* and *experience*. When people we admire demonstrate affection in their behavior, it is in itself a motivational factor to do the same thing. And the very *experience* of sharing affection in the context of acceptance and security also helps to develop this emotion.

Step B: We must acknowledge that there are some problems in the twentieth century that Scripture did not seem to deal with specifically. True, the Bible tells us what we *should* do, and in some instances gives us some clues as to *how* to do it. But in many instances, we must be creative within these basic guidelines.

For example, it is one thing for you to develop "feelings" of love for someone when you've never had these feelings before. But it is yet another problem if you once had "affectionate feelings" towards someone and then lost those feelings. To re-learn these feelings is far more difficult than to learn them the first time.

There were probably very few New Testament women who ever had this problem. Even though their situation was difficult they may never have had the experience, like Jane did, of falling out of love.

How can Jane develop these feelings again? Following are some suggested steps:

First, Jane should isolate why she feels the way she does. For example, is her husband insensitive? Does he not understand her needs? Is she "locked in" to a life of responsibility and boredom that she resents (and unconsciously blames her husband and takes it out on him)? Is she overburdened with responsibilities she can't handle by herself?

Question: What other reasons may there be for Jane's feelings?

Second, Jane must talk about her feelings and why they exist. Ideally, she should be able to communicate with her husband. If he is relatively mature spiritually and psychologically, he will listen without being overly threatened, even though it will be painful.

Note: Most men find it difficult to listen to their wives share feelings of unhappiness and resentment. It is very threatening. But the fact is, it is only as the husband learns to know what his wife's needs are that he can meet those needs. There *must* be communication.

Question: How can a wife communicate her negative feelings to her husband without overly threatening him?

Third, both Jane and Jim may need counseling from somebody else in the Body of Christ. This need not necessarily be "professional counseling" as we use this concept today. An older woman, for example, who is psychologically and spiritually mature can be of unusual help, especially to a younger woman who is having difficulty in these areas of her life. If Jane's and Jim's problems are unusually deep, however, they may both need professional counseling from someone who is trained in the area of helping people resolve marital conflicts.

Question: What additional suggestion do you feel needs to be made to help Jane (or someone like her) solve her problems?

Footnotes

1. The word used by Paul in Titus 2:4 is *philandros,* which is actually one word in the original Greek meaning "loving her husband."

2. The word *sophronizo* translated "train" in the *NIV* literally means to make one sober, to restore one to his senses; to moderate, control, curb, discipline; to admonish and exhort earnestly. The *NASB* reads, "that they may *encourage* the young women to love their husbands."

8 TO LOVE THEIR CHILDREN

"Likewise, teach the older women . . . then they can train the younger women to love their . . . children." *(Titus 2:3,4)*

Jim and Susan had been married for three years. By mutual consent they decided to postpone their family for about five years so Jim could complete graduate school and then become a fullfledged accountant.

Susan worked as an executive secretary. She loved her work and was making good money to help "put hubby through." She also took a few graduate courses at night school in the same university Jim attended. In fact, twice a week they met for dinner in the school cafeteria.

But then it happened: She became pregnant two years before their target date. Obviously, they had to change their plans radically. Susan dropped out of school immediately and then quit work during her sixth month of pregnancy.

She's now very much occupied at home as a young mother. Jim curtailed his study schedule drastically to earn enough money to care for his family. This meant postponing his graduation for a couple of years.

This story, of course, can be repeated many times in twentieth-century families. And it usually turns out quite well. Most people adapt, change their plans, and welcome into the world and their home a new personality.

But Jim and Susan's case is different. Immediately Susan sensed Jim's disappointment. She felt he blamed her for the pregnancy. And she had to admit her own disappointment. She resented having to drop out of school and give up her job, and down deep she resented Jim's attitude.

Today she has a persistent problem. Little Jim, Jr. is now two, and every day Susan fights feelings of resentment against her little boy. His daily needs and constant demands on her time are a persistent reminder of her earlier disappointment and negative feelings. To make matters worse, she feels guilty about resenting her son. All of this, of course, affects her relationship with her husband, Jim.

Mary's case is quite different. Ever since she can remember she looked forward to having children. She actually worked in the church nursery as a teenager because she loved babies.

But now, after four years of marriage, she has three of her own: ages one, two, and three. Beginning a family so soon and having one each year was actually her idea. Her husband, Bob, wanting to please her, certainly had no objections. But things are different now. Changing diapers in the church nursery was one thing; but to do it every day, several times a day, and for three children—well, that's another story. Her three demanding little personalities are beginning to drive her up the wall.

Bob isn't as understanding as he used to be, either. When he gets home from work, Mary is exhausted, the home is in shambles, and dinner isn't even started. To meet Bob's emotional and physical needs has become a real problem for Mary. By the end of the evening, she is so tired she falls asleep the moment her head hits the pillow, leaving Bob feeling neglected and rejected.

Actually Mary is beginning to resent Bob, blaming him for her predicament, even though it was her idea originally to have three children a year apart. Also, she's experiencing constant negative emotions toward the children. She finds herself resenting them deeply and blaming them for interfering with her ability to be a good wife to Bob. Furthermore, she feels she never has any time to herself, which is all too obvious. Her idealism has turned into a demanding routine that is leaving her frustrated, angry and, of course, guilty—which eventually ends up in depression.

Nancy's case is different yet. She has been married 20 years, and has four children, ages 9, 12, 15 and 17. Generally, she was a happy person, a good mother and very diligent as a housewife—until about three years ago. At that time she met a couple of friends who invited her to a special meeting to hear a woman speak on "Women's Rights."

Things she never really thought about before began to surface in her mind and emotions. Since that time, she has read articles, books, listened to more speakers, and is now convinced she is an unfulfilled woman. The reason, of course, revolved around her "wasted years."

She now resents the time spent with her children. In fact, she resents *them*. They are still dependent on her, which frustrates her no end. Obviously, they are interfering with her own desire to go back to school in order to prepare herself for a good job and a fulfilling position. Nancy is determined now that she is going to make up for lost time, no matter what happens to her family.

These three twentieth-century illustrations are based

on reality. True, they represent only three situations out of many and they vary in certain particulars when compared to real life situations. But in essence, they present three recurring problems in today's society. These women all have one thing in common; they are all having difficulty *feeling* love for their children. In fact, they all experience times of deep resentment.

A First-Century Problem, Too

The cultural situation in the New Testament world was far different than it is today. Not only were cultural situations different but the emotional dynamics were no doubt different. Yet women in those days likewise had difficulty loving their children. Thus Paul had to write to Titus, encouraging him to "teach the older women" to "train the younger women to *love . . . their children*" (Titus 2:3,4).

The phrase "to love their children" actually comes from one Greek word *(philoteknos)*, which literally means to be "child-lovers." As in our previous study on learning to "love their husbands," Paul again uses *phileo* love which definitely includes the emotional dimensions in human relationships. These women in New Testament days were to learn to "love their children"; that is, to have positive feelings toward their offspring.

They probably had difficulty loving their children for the same reasons they had difficulty loving their husbands. A child born as a result of "dutiful performance" doesn't set a very good stage for a love relationship between mother and children. A wife's resentment towards her husband can easily extend to their children.

We must also remember that women in the first century were really little different in their emotional makeup than women in the twentieth century. The cultural factors certainly alter our emotional nature, yet human beings are constructed pretty much the same all over the world. In other words, resentments towards children may have emerged from varying reasons in the first-century world, but the emotional reactions were probably pretty much the same. What a woman "feels today" is pretty much what she "felt then."

Some Practical Guidelines

How can a woman learn "to love her children"? What practical suggestions and guidelines are there for developing this capacity?

1. Realize that negative feelings under certain circumstances are normal, even for mature Christian women. The pressures of family life, particularly when children are young, are very real. Life with small children in the home is wall to wall, literally involving 24 hours a day. At no other time and in no other situation will there be as much physical and emotional drain on a mother. And this is complicated and intensified by the fact that this is a new role for her. Innately she takes her responsibility very seriously and, as a Christian, her natural sense of responsibility becomes even more acute through her knowledge of biblical expectations. There is no more threatening thought to a young woman than the prospect of being a failure as a mother. And most face this mental obsession sometime during the early years of motherhood.

We must also realize that physical strain has a tendency to make a person vulnerable to emotional difficulties. Furthermore, emotional stress invariably leads to feelings of resentment. And for a Christian particularly, hostile emotions lead to guilt and depression, which in turn creates a vicious cycle leading to more guilt and recurring depression.

Every young woman must understand these pressures and the natural tendency toward resentment. To have periodic negative emotions and feel resentment toward young children in the home is normal. Generally it does not mean a "lack of real love" for the child, any more than experiencing periodic negative emotions toward her husband means she doesn't really love him. To understand these emotions and why they are occurring helps a person to accept the feelings, and to avoid the nagging guilt which inevitably makes the problem worse.

It goes without saying, though it *must* be said, that a young husband *must* understand his wife's struggles in this area. If he is threatened, feels rejected, and becomes insensitive, and then vents his own emotional frustration on her, he will only compound her anxiety and depression. She must have a listening ear from the one who is closest to her.

2. Young women need help from older women. This is why Paul told Titus to "teach the *older women*" to "train the *younger women*." And this is why he emphasized the older woman's example in this process. Young women need mature adult models. And they need insight that is helpful, not harmful.

Unfortunately, some older women forget what it was like to go through these early years of motherhood. And some develop an idealism that is far removed from reality. Rather than easing the burden of anxiety and guilt by letting the young woman know they experienced the same emotions, they accentuate the problem by telling them "not to feel that way," and by giving the impression that mature people don't have these problems.

First of all, you cannot change a person's feelings by telling them *not to feel that way*. And second, it doesn't help to give the impression these feelings are abnormal. And third, it is dishonest for an older woman to give the impression she never had these difficulties when indeed she really did.

Note: If you happen to be an older woman who never

experienced negative feelings towards your small children, you are the exception, not the rule. If indeed you did not have these feelings, there were probably some very significant reasons why this was true: a very understanding husband, unusual help from someone else in carrying out the process, a completely different environment and cultural milieu, etc. If you are going to be a good counselor you must understand why your experience deviated from the norm.

3. Realize more than ever that cultural trends can be devastating to family life. Nancy, of course, is a good example of this. She was basically happy and contented with her role until she began to associate with women who convinced her she was "unfulfilled." And indeed, she began to *feel* unfulfilled. The more she read the writings of "unhappy" women, the more she identified with their plight and the more she began to *feel* like them.

The women's liberation movement, of course, is only one trend in our culture that has made devastating inroads into the average American family. Combined with this are the trends of secularism, materialism, sensualism, and existentialism. Everywhere a woman turns she is bombarded with a value system that is eating away at what God ordained to be a very fulfilling and rewarding lifestyle.

4. Develop a biblical perspective on motherhood. The Bible clearly teaches that children are a "gift of the Lord" (Ps. 127:3, *NASB*), and personally, I believe the Scriptures teach that having children is one of God's major plans for women to experience fulfillment. Thus Paul, when discussing the effects of the fall on woman's status in life (see 1 Tim. 2:11-15), wrote something that is rather difficult to understand out of context. He said, "But woman will be kept safe through childbirth, if they continue in faith, love and holiness with propriety" (1 Tim. 2:15).

What Paul meant by this statement has been the subject of a lot of discussion. Obviously, he did not mean a woman finds eternal salvation through producing children. This would be totally contradictory to the whole of Scripture. Rather it seems he is saying that a woman, though she has been affected negatively by the fall, being the first one to sin and though she must recognize man's authority in her life, yet, her most significant fulfillment will come by being a good wife and mother.

If she turns her life totally over to God, she can be "saved" from the competitive problems in a male-dominated culture—men whose male egos are also desperately affected by sin in the world. She will be "saved" from the loneliness and frustration that often accompany a career. She will be "saved" from the pressures of a rat-race culture, having someone who will understand and help her find fulfillment.

We must hurry to add, of course, that this doesn't mean a woman cannot be fulfilled without having children or a husband. In fact, Paul commends singlehood for those who feel led this way. The point is that many in today's world are attempting to communicate that having children, being a wife and mother can *never* lead to fulfillment. This, of course, is in direct contradiction to the Scriptures and runs counter to God's principles.

5. *Realize, however, that culture does create new problems for women.* We cannot ignore culture. Young girls in our society are taught to be professionally oriented throughout their academic experiences. The concept of parenting takes a decided backseat to the excitement of a professional career.

Psychologically, most women are geared in a direction other than what God intended. And this means that all of us, both men and women, must understand the influence culture has on our personalities. To simply "put a woman down" or "to put her in her place" may accentuate her problem. She needs to *understand* her problem. She must realize her tendency is to act the way she has been subtly conditioned to act. Together, a husband and wife must face the reality of this problem and, within the context of Christian principles, work toward a satisfactory solution.

A Personal or Group Project

Step A: Utilizing these five guidelines, evaluate each of the three illustrations at the beginning of this lesson. Use them as case studies. What suggestions would you give Susan for solving her problem? What suggestions would you give Mary? And how would you counsel Nancy? Be specific.

Step B: What about your own personal experience—either as an older woman whose children are grown, or as a younger woman who is in the process of rearing children? What can you do to carry out Paul's directive?

Step C: What can a mature single woman do to help carry out Paul's directive?

9 TO BE
SELF-CONTROLLED

"Likewise, teach the older women . . . then they can train the younger women . . . to be self-controlled."
(Titus 2:3-5)

No quality of life stands out more boldly in Scripture as a mark of Christian maturity than being "self-controlled." In our Scripture text for this chapter, Paul said to challenge *young women* to be self-controlled. But he also mentioned it in two other places as a quality for elders (see 1 Tim. 3:2; Titus 1:8). In another place in Scripture he exhorted both *older men* and *young men* to be self-controlled (Titus 2:2, 6).

Writing to Timothy, his fellow-missionary and an often fearful young man, Paul encouraged him with these words, "For God did not give us a spirit of timidity, but a spirit of power, of love and of *self-discipline*" or self-control (2 Tim. 1:7). And after using the word four times in his letter to Titus to help present a "profile for a Christian life-style" for all ages and both sexes (see Titus 1:8; 2:2,5,6), Paul culminated this section of his letter with an exhortation to the *whole* body of believers in Crete. Appealing to God's marvelous grace, he wrote, "It teaches us to say, 'No' to ungodliness and worldy passions, and to live *self-controlled,*, upright, and godly lives in this present age" (Titus 2:12).

What does it mean to be self-controlled? The basic English word describing this quality of life is translated from various forms of the word in the Greek text. But in most instances the meaning is similar, both in its primary and secondary definitions. It has to do with being "sensible," "sober," and of a "sound mind." It describes a person who is in control of his physical, and psychological, and spiritual faculties. He is not in bondage to his desires, impulses, and passions.

Some Twentieth-Century Applications

What did Paul really mean when he exhorted older women to "train"[1] younger women to be self-controlled? Let's look at some twentieth-century applications of some first-century exhortations.

From the first day Jane arrived on the scene, everyone got the distinct impression she felt she was God's gift to the Body of Christ. Everyone she talked to quickly heard about her participation and achievements in other Christian circles. She sang solos, played the piano, and taught a variety of Sunday School classes and, the clincher, she knew Billy Graham *personally* (which being interpreted means she managed to maneuver herself into a receiving line on one occasion when he was greeting people and shook his hand).

Don't misunderstand! There is nothing wrong in taking the opportunity to meet a well-known Christian. The point is that Jane was "name-dropping" in a dishonest way ("I know Billy Graham personally") to impress other people.

Paul spoke to this issue in his letter to the Romans:

"By the grace given to me I say to every one of you: Do not think of yourself more highly than *you ought,* but rather think of yourself with *sober judgment* [literally: be sober-minded], in accordance with the measure of faith God has given you" (Rom. 12:3). Here Paul used the basic Greek word that is often translated "self-controlled" in other scriptural texts.[2]

Evidently, some of the Roman Christians were, like the Corinthians, using their spiritual gifts and abilities to put other Christians down. Paul had to remind them that everyone in the Body of Christ is important, even those who are less prominent personalities.

Jane's problem has at least two possible explanations. On the one hand, she may have been in the limelight all her life. This experience created a psychological need to perform and to be recognized. On the other hand, she may have been deprived of love and attention as a youngster. This led her to "put herself down." Now she feels she has to compensate by striving for personal achievement that competes with others. But whatever the source of the problem, the outer manifestation is pride and lack of self-control in this area of her life. What she needs, implied Paul, is a good parental model, preferably an older godly woman, who is sensitive and who can help Jane understand her problem and become more Christlike in her behavior.

Mary's problem is the opposite of Jane's, at least in its outward manifestation. She constantly withdraws from others and feels inferior. When other people reach out to her, she feels uncomfortable. She's afraid she'll say the wrong thing and cause them to dislike her.

In certain respects Timothy's problem seems to be similar to Mary's. He was no doubt timid and fearful. Thus Paul had to encourage him with these words, "For God did not give us a spirit of timidity [fear], but a spirit of power, of love and of self-discipline" or self-control (2 Tim. 1:7).

Timothy had nothing to be ashamed of. He had a good heritage—a weak father perhaps, but a godly mother and grandmother (see 2 Tim. 1:5; 3:14,15). He was one of God's choice servants, a fellow-missionary with the great Apostle Paul. Paul personally called Timothy into the ministry (see Acts 16:3) and became the instrument by which God bestowed an unusual spiritual gift on this young man (see 2 Tim. 1:6).[3] There was no reason for Timothy to be timid and fearful. Yet he was! And throughout his life he needed constant encouragement to live boldly for God. Some feel his stomach problems referred to in 1 Timothy 5:23 were the result of emotional difficulties; that is, his fear and timid personality.

Mary, too, needs encouragement. Paul implied in his letter to Titus that a godly older woman who is mature in this area of her life can serve as the best means to help Mary overcome her inferiority complex. In short, she needs godly, feminine models.

At this point, we can gain a helpful insight from psychology. Children who make improper identifications in the early years of their life often have difficulty "finding themselves," or really knowing "who they are." For example, a young girl about age three begins the process of identifying with her mother, taking on feminine qualities. As she grows and enters her teen years, the need for a proper feminine model becomes even more necessary. When this process is missing, it frequently affects her ability in later life to develop a proper self-image. This is no doubt one reason why the Holy Spirit guided Paul to emphasize that older women were to help younger women to develop certain qualities in their lives. Obviously, many of these young women lacked the proper models as they were growing up in their pagan homes.

Barbara and Cynthia are sisters. Their problem is similar, but also different. Both are newly married. Both have focused on material things to attract attention to themselves—but in different ways.

Barbara dresses extravagantly, often driving her husband to a state of anger and rebellion. She spends money beyond their means, buying expensive clothes and jewelry she wears only a few times and on rare occasions. Her desire to impress other people, particularly other women, seems almost insatiable.

Cynthia's problem, though related to Barbara's in its roots, manifests itself somewhat differently. She, too, is obsessed with impressing others, but the objects of her attention-getting behavior are men. She is extravagant in her spending, but her grooming habits concentrate on being seductive. She knows she can get the eye of every red-blooded man and she consciously schemes to achieve that goal. Obviously, she threatens her husband desperately. She is very cold and insensitive towards him at home, yet in public she acts seductively toward him as well as other men.

Paul warned Christian women against this kind of behavior. "I also want women," he wrote, "to dress modestly, with decency and *propriety* [that is, with self-control and personal discipline], not with braided hair or gold or pearls or expensive clothes, but with good deeds, appropriate for women who profess to worship God" (1. Tim. 2:9).

Don't misunderstand! Paul is not saying a woman should not make herself beautiful. What he is warning against is materialistic behavior that is based on self-centered attitudes. He is speaking to women who are not self-controlled in this area of their lives. They don't use good sense. Their personal needs for attention are so strong that they lose perspective, even in the area of Christian morality and what is indeed "appropriate for women who profess to worship God."

Both Barbara and Cynthia were neglected as children. When all other little girls wore pretty dresses and experienced normal acceptance and praise, they stood out as being different. Now they're compensating, one in one way and the other in another way. But the results are the same emotionally. They "feel" they are getting the attention they lacked as children.

By biblical standards both actions are wrong even though they have psychological roots. Both Barbara and Cynthia need to become self-controlled, to become godly women who are mature in Jesus Christ. And again, they need the example of older Christian women who can train them to develop this quality.

A Personal or Group Project

The following project is designed to help you as a Christian woman develop self-control.

Step A: Though the illustrations used in this chapter are extreme, they may surface elements of carnality in your own Christian life-style and also give you insights into your own personal motivations. At this point, re-read the illustrations. Reflect and note any correlation between your own behavior and what you've read.

Note: These illustrations are specific. There are other reasons why people react in these ways and there are other behavioral manifestations, some conscious and other unconscious.

Questions:

1. What other *reasons* may cause a woman (a) to put others down, (b) to withdraw, or (c) to attract attention to herself?

2. What other *ways* do problems of this nature manifest themselves?

Step B: If you identify with any of these problems,

look for an older woman who can serve as a guiding model and interpreter. Ask the Lord to direct you to that kind of person.

Warning: It is easy to get our eyes off Jesus Christ and on people who will disappoint us. Remember that not all older women who appear to have it together spiritually and emotionally really do so. No human being is perfect, so don't look for the ideal individual. In fact, some people who are the most honest about their imperfections can be the most help. But remember, idealism, towards ourselves and others, always leads to disappointment. This is why it is important to realize that only Jesus Christ is the same yesterday, today, and forever.

Questions:

1. What kind of model are you to women younger than you are?

2. If you are a mother, what kind of model are you to your daughter or daughters? What are they learning from your life-style—your attitude toward God, toward your husband, toward your home, toward your neighbors and other Christians?

Step C: Think through some specific suggestions you might give Jane to help her solve her problems. Do the same for Mary, Barbara, and Cynthia.

A Final Thought

Peter wrote, "The end of all things is near. Therefore be *clear minded* and *self-controlled* so that you can pray" (1 Pet. 4:7).

Footnotes

1. Significantly, the Greek word *sophronizo,* which is a member of the family of words translated "self-control" in the *NIV,* is the basic word translated "they can train" in Titus 2:4. In other words, the very essence of the process of "training" young women to love their husbands and children, to be self-controlled and pure, to be busy at home, to be kind, to be subject to their husbands, relates to the very word under the discussion in this chapter. *Sophronizo* (to train) means to make one *sophron* (self-controlled). It means to restore one to his senses; to moderate, control, curb, discipline. In other words, older women who are "self-controlled" would then be able through the very process of being "self-controlled" to enable younger women to *become* "self-controlled."
2. Compare specifically Romans 12:3 with Titus 2:6, "Similarly, encourage the younger men to be *self-controlled.*"
3. We don't know for sure what Timothy's gift was, though it was miraculously given to him when Paul laid his hands on him. From the context of 2 Timothy 1:3-7, it may have been a special gift of faith. Or from the general context of the pastoral epistles written to Timothy, it may have been a special gift of teaching and/or pastoring.

10 TO BE PURE

"Likewise, teach the older women . . . then they can train the younger women . . . to be self-controlled and pure." (Titus 2:3-5)

Purity, particularly in sexual matters, stands out on the pages of the Bible as a hallmark of Christian maturity. And this is no doubt what Paul had in mind when he instructed older women to train younger women to be "pure." The Greek word *hagnos* literally means to be pure from carnality; to be chaste; to be modest.

The culture of Paul's day was noted for its immorality. Men particularly lived according to their sensual impulses and, as in our twentieth-century culture, women were always available. What men wanted, they usually got! These women in Paul's day, just as they are today, were no doubt motivated more by emotional needs than physical impulses, but the end result was immorality and impurity.

A Biblical Emphasis
The subjects emphasized by biblical writers reflect the

major problems in New Testament churches, and no problem is dealt with more consistently than immorality. Hardly a letter was penned that did not treat this subject specifically, graphically, and with candor.

Timothy, who was a young unmarried pastor, evidently faced numerous opportunities for illicit sexual involvements; there were plenty of "available" women. Consequently, Paul cautioned this young man to always "set an example for the believers in speech, in life, in love, in faith and in *purity*" (1 Tim. 4:12). And when it came to women his own age, Paul minced no words: Treat "younger women as sisters, with *absolute purity*" (1 Tim. 5:2). And just to make sure Timothy really understood the seriousness of this matter and how quickly any man, no matter how spiritual he may be, can fall prey to sexual temptation, he restated his concern a few lines later in the very same letter; *"Keep yourself* pure!" warned Paul (1 Tim. 5:22).

There is plenty of biblical evidence to demonstrate that Timothy was a very sensitive young man, both emotionally and physically. And like King David, who also evidenced similar personality traits, he was vulnerable sexually. A man who has a warm heart towards God also usually has a warm heart toward people; and a man's warm heart toward people generally may become a *very* warm heart toward women particularly, especially during times of loneliness and inactivity. What may be a *pure motive* initially can oftentimes lead to *impure actions*.

Paul was concerned that *all* Christian women, young and old alike, realize their responsibility in maintaining pure relationships with men. In many respects women's attitudes and behavior are more determinative than men. Though they may be classified in some respects as the "weaker" person, when it comes to sexual power and control they are definitely stronger. History is filled with accounts of men who, though rulers over kingdoms and people, were often under the spell of beautiful and sensual women.

Consider King Herod of Jesus' day. He was living with his brother Philip's wife, Herodias, whose own scheming no doubt played a significant part in this very open but illegitimate relationship. John the Baptist spoke out boldly against this immoral arrangement. "It is not lawful for you to have her," he cried out boldly to Herod and for everyone to hear (see Matt. 14:4).

Herod was embarrassed, but not nearly as much as Herodias was, who "nursed a grudge against John." In fact, she "wanted to kill him." But as Mark records, "she was not able to, because Herod feared John and protected him, knowing him to be a righteous and holy man" (Mark 6:19,20).

But Herodias' hatred gave birth to an evil scheme that cost John his head. Her opportunity came one evening when Herod was under the influence of Herodias' beautiful daughter who performed a sensuous dance for all the leading men of Galilee—high officials, military commanders and other notables. It was Herod's birthday, and no doubt the combination of evil involvement, alcohol and lust caused him to promise Herodias' daughter anything her heart desired—up to half of his kingdom.

At that moment Herodias moved into action (the scheme she devised was right on target). She prompted her daughter, gross as it was, to ask for John the Baptist's head on a platter. Herod, though a ruler of many people, because of his pride, his weakness and his bondage to a sensual and evil woman, gave an order for John to be killed (see Matt. 14:1-12; Mark 6:14-29).

How tragic! But how true. Women's sexual favors have brought men of all walks of life to their knees, and caused them to give up fame, fortune, and position.

Tony was such a person. At one time he was in Chris-

tian work. He and his lovely wife were getting up in years.
He met a young girl, many years younger than himself
who obviously needed a father image, and he needed the
ego satisfaction she could give him with her sexual favors.
Consequently, he left his wife, disillusioned his children,
and openly lied to those who confronted him with his sin.
Spiritually he turned his back on everything he stood for.
Psychologically he was like putty in this young woman's
hand. Mentally his thinking became bizarre and irrational.
It was as if he were under a hypnotic spell.

In some respects this is ironic. The Bible teaches that
man is to be the stronger, the leader, the one in charge and
in control. Woman is to be in submission, in a position
offering respect and honor. But underneath it all, God did
not take away from woman the ultimate power over
men—sex. Used in selfish and sinful ways, she has the
potential to consistently manipulate man to her own advantage. This Paul warned against. By all means, it should
never be a part of the life-style of a Christian woman.
Thus Paul instructed Titus to "teach the older women to
. . . train the younger women . . . to be self-controlled and
pure."

The apostle Peter dealt with the issue of purity when
writing to women who were married to non-Christian husbands. "Be submissive to your husbands" he wrote, "so
that, if any of them do not believe the word, they may be
won over without talk by the behavior of their wives,
when they see the *purity* and reverence of your lives" (1
Pet. 3:1,2).

Knowing Christ as Saviour was to bring significant life-
style changes, particularly in the area of moral values. And
though an unbelieving husband in those days may have
continued to be morally lax, Peter instructed wives who
became believers to demonstrate marital faithfulness and
purity. This, combined with "submission," and the "unfad-

ing beauty of a gentle and quiet spirit," oftentimes became a means whereby an unsaved husband became a Christian.

Though the Scriptures do not guarantee that this approach will always work, in more instances than not it does, even in the twentieth century, especially if a woman consistently and patiently practices these principles. There is inherent in man a tendency to respond to a woman who respects him, who is loyal to him, and who practices the presence of Jesus Christ. This kind of behavior the Bible condones as legitimate influence and control. Though it may take time, the results are frequently forthcoming.

Jane's experience verifies this Scriptural truth. She was converted to Christ in a woman's home Bible study. Both she and her husband Jim had been on the cocktail circuit and were "swinging" with a very loose crowd. Since a lot of their friends were periodically swapping mates, they joined in the crowd. Though not particularly appealing to Jane, even as a non-Christian, she went along with her friends.

When Jane became a Christian she did so knowing her previous life-style was out of tune with Christian values. The Bible class teacher helped her to focus in on Peter's instruction in his first epistle. Jane began immediately to practice this principle.

At first her husband Jim was skeptical, even resentful. But the superficiality of his life-style, viewed against the reality and depth of Jane's new life-style, eventually convinced him of the reality of Christianity. Today Jim is also a Christian, and their life together has never been richer and more fulfilling.

A Personal or Group Project

The following personal project is designed to help you, as a Christian woman, evaluate your behavior in the light of what the Bible teaches is proper and acceptable in the area of moral purity.

Step A: Recognize, first of all, that sexual power is a gift of God and like any other gift, it can be used appropriately or inappropriately. God's plan is that it be used to benefit others within His will for mankind. Consider the following guidelines:

1. Ultimate sexual expression between a man and a woman is to take place within the bonds of legitimate and recognized marriage. Any other relationship is out of the will of God and is classified as a violation of His moral law. In short, it is sin (see Gen. 2:23-25).

Note: A marriage that follows biblical examples and principles involves life commitment to one person, parental involvement and blessing, and obedience to the laws and legal codes of a particular culture or community.

2. Ultimate sexual expression within a legitimate marriage is designed by God and is a part of His plan for a man and a woman. In fact, when either marriage partner refuses to meet the sexual needs of the other partner, that person is violating God's will (see 1 Cor. 7:1-5).

Note: There are other instructions in Scripture that add additional perspective to the above guideline. For example, a relationship between a Christian man and woman is to be governed by an attitude of unselfishness, humility, and self-sacrifice (see Eph. 5:22-33). This is important, because some individuals use Paul's statement in 1 Corinthians 7 as a right to make excessive demands upon their marriage partner that are definitely improper and out of harmony with the spirit of love that reflects Jesus Christ.

3. Ultimately sexual expression is designed by God to be more than a means of procreation. Rather, it is also an expression of love, concern, and unity. In addition, it is also a means of meeting physical and psychological needs.

And it is to be pleasurable and fun. For God's viewpoint on the enjoyable aspects of sex, read the Song of Solomon.

4. God designed sex to be one of the most creative experiences a man and a woman can have together. He sets no restrictions on the way it is expressed, other than it is always to be a mutual expression of Christlike love. Whatever is acceptable between a man and a woman who are married is within His will and blessing. Only culture sets restrictions, not God.

5. God has definitely given woman a sexual power over man. Her unique physical beauty, her feminine charms, her ability to give physical pleasure in a variety of ways, her capacity to provide emotional security—all of these abilities should be used by her to their fullest capacity in order to help her husband be a fulfilled person.

Note: God has also designed that when a woman fulfills her God-ordained role, she will, in turn, be a fulfilled person. Obviously, there are exceptions to this rule, but generally, it works out as God planned.

6. On the other hand, a woman's sexual powers are to be definitely restrictive and used exclusively in relationship to her husband. With all other men she is to be discreet and modest. In no way should she deliberately or even naively attract men to herself sexually. To do so is to violate Paul's instructions to be "pure."

Step B: Evaluate your behavior in the light of these biblical guidelines. The following questions will help you:

1. Am I consistently meeting my husband's emotional and sexual needs, helping to minimize the temptations that he faces in a world of women who deliberately use their sexual power to attract men to themselves sexually?

2. Do I as a woman (either single or married) avoid attracting men to myself sexually? Am I discreet and modest in what I wear, particularly covering up the parts of my body that God designed to be sexually attractive and stim-

ulating to a man within the bonds of marriage?

Note: We must recognize that there is a certain cultural relativity in determining what is proper and improper in dress. According to Solomon, a woman in her totality can be sexually stimulating (see Song of Sol. 4:1-15). However, cultural trends enhance certain parts of the body. At this point, a Christian woman must be discreet and sensitive, never using her cultural freedom to violate biblical principles. Whatever behavior creates sexual problems for men generally is improper.

3. Do I understand sufficiently the sexual nature of a normal man, that is, how he functions mentally, emotionally, and physically? And do I use this information properly in marriage to enhance the relationship and outside of marriage to avoid creating temptations and problems for other men?

4. Do I have any psychological and spiritual problems that are causing me to behave improperly toward other men?

For example, here are some obvious manifestations of some root problems. Mary behaves very seductively towards men but is very cold towards her husband. Joan consistently wears clothing that reveals her breasts. Sara makes a point of wearing unusually short skirts and deliberately crosses her legs in the presence of men. June habitually wears clothing that enhances her natural body curves. Katy persistently reaches out and touches men. Judy regularly uses endearing terms around men that ordinarily are personal, such as calling men "love," "dear," "sweetie," "precious," "sugar," etc.

Note: Some of these symptoms of course, reflect naiveté. But generally they reflect deeper problems in a woman's personality. In some instances they are not aware of the root problems, but generally they are very cognizant of what they are doing.

Step C: Following are some additional paragraphs taken from Paul's letters warning against improper sexual behavior. Study these Scriptures carefully, and make sure your own life-style measures up to God's standards.

• "Let us behave decently, as in the daytime, not in orgie and drunkenness, not in sexual immorality and debauchery, not in dissension and jealousy. Rather, clothe yourselves with the Lord Jesus Christ, and do not think about how to gratify the desires of your sinful nature" (Rom. 13:13,14).

• "Flee from sexual immorality. All other sins a man commits are outside his body, but he who sins sexually sins against his own body. Do you not know that your body is a temple of the Holy Spirit, who is in you, whom you have received from God? You are not your own; you were bought at a price. Therefore honor God with your body" (1 Cor. 6:18-20).

• "But if you are led by the Spirit, you are not under law. The acts of the sinful nature are obvious: sexual immorality, impurity and debauchery; idolatry and witchcraft; hatred, discord, jealousy, fits of rage, selfish ambition, dissensions, factions and envy; drunkenness, orgies, and the like. I warn you, as I did before, that those who live like this will not inherit the kingdom of God" (Gal. 5:18-21).

• "And this is my prayer: that your love may abound more and more in knowledge and depth of insight, so that you may be able to discern what is best and may be pure and blameless until the day of Christ, filled with the fruit of righteousness that comes through Jesus Christ—to the glory and praise of God" (Phil. 1:9-11).

• "Put to death, therefore, whatever belongs to your earthly nature: sexual immorality, impurity, lust, evil desires and greed, which is idolatry. Because of these, the wrath of God is coming. You used to walk in these ways, in the life you once lived. But now you must rid yourselves of all such things as these: anger, rage, malice, slander, filthy language" (Col. 3:5-8).

• "Marriage should be honored by all, and the marriage bed kept pure, for God will judge the adulterer and all the sexually immoral" (Heb. 13:4).

11 TO BE
BUSY
AT HOME

"Likewise, teach the older women . . . then they can train the younger women . . . to be busy at home." (Titus 2:3-5)

In a day when the philosophy of Women's Liberation has penetrated and influenced the thinking of many Christian women, Paul's injunction to be "busy at home" may well be one of the most controversial subjects in this book. In fact, there are some "Bible-believing Christians" who interpret certain of Paul's statements about women as being heavily influenced and biased by his own Jewish environment and culture, thus making them no longer relevant and authoritative in the twentieth century.

This poses some unusual problems in Bible interpretation. In fact, it opens up a very serious area for discussion regarding the inspiration and authority of the Bible. If Paul was in error regarding the role of women, what about all the other subjects he wrote about? In fact, if Paul was in error about women, who's to say he wasn't in error regarding how a man is saved?

Personally, I believe Paul was inspired by the Holy Spirit to write *all* that he wrote. And though there are certain issues he dealt with that were purely local and cultural, even regarding women, there is no way to interpret his general teaching about women's roles in this way without raising serious questions about the authority of the Bible. And one of these teachings that is certainly normative for all times is that a mature godly woman—in this case a married woman—will be "busy at home." This concept is consistent with the whole of Scripture from Genesis to Revelation.

What Paul Does Not Mean

One of the major reasons Paul has been under fire from a variety of critics lies in the fact that he has been misinterpreted, both by Bible-believing Christians and non-Christians. Often this misinterpretation by Christians creates the greatest misunderstandings among non-Christians. Many unbelievers assume that what some Christians *believe* Paul was saying is indeed *what he was saying* and they quickly conclude that the Bible is an outdated and outmoded book. It is very important, then, to first of all clarify what Paul did *not* mean when he said women are to be "busy at home."

When Paul instructed younger women to be "busy at home" he was not teaching that a woman could not be active outside the home, even pursuing a professional career. If he were, he certainly would be contradicting what the Scriptures describe as an "excellent wife" in Proverbs 31:10-27. In this passage, in addition to the many "home responsibilities," she is presented as a woman who is involved in real estate investments (v. 16) and who has her own manufacturing business (v. 24).

Some people (men particularly) have interpreted Paul's injunction to mean that a woman must do all the work by herself. Some men will never lift a finger to help with the housework since "this is the wife's God-ordained responsibility."

There is nothing in the Bible to support this kind of behavior. It reflects subjective reasoning and makes the Bible teach something it does not teach. In fact, the Bible teaches the opposite. A Christian man is to love his wife as Christ loved the church, which means demonstrating an attitude of unselfishness, humility, and sensitivity (see Phil. 2:5-8; 1 Pet. 3:7). In essence, a godly husband has a servant's heart (see Phil. 2:7).

Some Christian men, of course, extend this concept to include never allowing their wives to secure help with their housework. This, of course, runs counter to many biblical situations, because many wives in both the Old Testament and New Testament had servants to help them with their responsibilities. In fact, the woman described in Proverbs 31 no doubt had a number of servants and helpers.

This, of course, is not to advocate extending or promoting the concept of "slavery." Not so! But there is nothing in the Bible that says it is *improper* for a woman whose home responsibilities are unusually heavy to hire someone to help her with her work. Obviously, of course, the family's financial income has a great deal to do with whether or not this is a possibility.

Because of some of Paul's direct statements about a woman's role, some have interpreted that he is classifying women as second-class citizens. But they forget that the same man who wrote, "Neither was man created for woman, but woman for man" (1 Cor. 11:9), also wrote, "there is neither Jew nor Greek, nor slave nor free, *male nor female,* for you are *all one* in Christ Jesus" (Gal. 3:28).

In God's sight, a woman's spiritual position in Christ is no different than a man's. In fact they are as one. There are no sexual distinctions. However, as we'll see, God has established some temporal and functional roles for women, especially because of the principle of sin that is operative in the world. But this in no way makes them second-class citizens. In short, being a homemaker is not a menial task that is second in importance to being a breadwinner. Furthermore, this God-ordained role need not restrict her in accomplishing other tasks.

Some Christian women suffer from an inferiority complex. Unfortunately, much of this is due to an improper view of themselves because of incorrect biblical teaching. To concentrate on a woman's functional roles in the church and home as described by Paul (and other New Testament writers) without balancing these statements with what is written about her position in Christ will lead to incorrect conclusions. And when these imbalances are taught to women, one of two things often happens. Either they reject what they believe the Bible teaches and set out to prove they are just as capable as men (frequently in angry and aggressive ways), or they accept what they have been taught as "gospel truth" and consider themselves inferior to men.

The fact is that women are not inferior to men, particularly in the realm of intellectual and psychological capabilities. True, they are the "weaker vessels" in terms of physical strength, but this must never be classified as synonymous with being inferior. Some of the greatest literary, artistic, and scientific achievements have been accomplished by women. Though the Scriptures place definite restrictions on their behavior in order to maintain proper role relationships, it does not mean a woman is not capable of great achievements, even within the boundaries God has laid out for her. And being "busy at home" in no way need stand in the way of demonstrating her creative potential, even in realms outside of the home.

What Paul Does Mean

What does Paul mean when he instructs young women to be "busy at home?" A quick look at the context in which Paul makes this statement makes it very clear that he is talking about married women who are to "love their husbands and children." He is also concerned that these women be "self-controlled and pure" (Titus 2:3-5).

Paul had the same concern for young widows in Ephesus who got "into the habit of being idle and going about from house to house. And," wrote Paul, "not only do they become idlers, but also gossips and busybodies, saying things they ought not to." Consequently, Paul counseled these young women "to marry, to have children, and to *manage their homes* and to give the enemy no opportunity for slander" (1 Tim. 5:13,14).

In other words, Paul is dealing with a woman's priorities. In the New Testament culture particularly, a woman found it difficult to function productively outside the context of family life. She had very little to do other than get into difficulty, particularly moral difficulty. Consequently, Paul advised these young women to marry or, if they were married, to avoid being "busy" in places other than within their homes.

Fortunately, this is not true in many twentieth-century situations. Single women (and married women alike) often have opportunities to function in responsible jobs and roles that provide them with positive and rewarding experiences.

But what Paul is saying here is more than cultural. In fact, there is a supracultural and divine principle inherent in marriage and family life that provides a woman with significant fulfillment. As stated before, I believe Paul treats this principle in what has often been classified as an obscure passage in his first letter to Timothy. "A woman should learn in quietness and full submission. I do not permit a woman to teach or to have authority over a man; she must be silent. For Adam was first formed, then Eve. And Adam was not the one deceived; it was the woman who was deceived and became a sinner. But," and this is the significant statement, "women will be kept safe through childbirth if they continue in faith, love, and holiness with propriety" (1 Tim. 2:11-15).

What could Paul possibly mean by this final statement? There have been many interpretations. I believe that Paul is talking about the fulfillment a woman can discover by being a good wife and mother. But note: it is not just being a wife and mother that brings fulfillment, but being a woman of "faith, love, and holiness"; in other words, a *Christian* wife and mother. Herein lies the supracultural dimension. God has ordained that a woman can find her greatest fulfillment and sense of accomplishment in rearing a family that follows after God. To resist this process is to work against the divine principle established by the God of the universe.

In summary, then, when a woman chooses to be a wife and mother she chooses a definite God-ordained role. Since the beginning of creation, and particularly after the fall, God's plan is that a married woman's priority is to be her home. Her husband's priority is to be the provider. God confirmed this arrangement after the fall when He said that in pain, Eve was to bear children and by the sweat of his face, Adam was to provide for his family (Gen. 3:16-19).

But God gave us a partial escape from the lingering effects of sin in this life. He gave it in His guidelines for marriage and family life. Ultimately, He will deliver us totally from the sin of Adam and Eve. But in the meantime, He provides fulfillment and reward for the husband and wife who are living in His will.

A married woman who wants to be in the will of God,

then, will make her home a priority. This is Paul's message to Timothy. This is what he means. Even though God allows a great deal of freedom as to how she does this, the important thing is that she does it. If she does not, her marriage and family life is headed for serious problems. She cannot violate a biblical principle without suffering the natural consequences.

A Personal or Group Project

The following project is designed to help you as a Christian woman evaluate your behavior in the light of what the Bible says regarding marital and family life.

Step A: If you are a single woman, recognize that being single need not interfere with the sense of fulfillment described in this chapter. It is true that a single woman who is living in a marriage-conscious society may feel cheated. It is possible that she will fall into the trap of introspection and loneliness, which in turn can lead to anxiety and even bitterness. But it need not happen, particularly in a culture that provides her so many opportunities for fulfillment in other legitimate ways.

One outstanding illustration of a single woman called of God to a life of fruitful service is the late Dr. Henrietta Mears. Of her, Dr. Billy Graham said, "She has had a remarkable influence, both directly and indirectly, on my life. In fact, I doubt if any other woman outside of my wife and mother has had such a marked influence . . . . She is certainly one of the greatest Christians I have ever known."[1]

Her influence was also significant in the life of Bill Bright, the founder of Campus Crusade for Christ. Bill was a member of the college group she taught and it was in her home that Campus Crusade was launched.

Under her dynamic leadership as director of Christian education at the Hollywood Presbyterian Church, the Sunday School enrollment grew from 450 to 4,200 in two and one-half years—an average weekly gain of over 30 people per Sunday. Out of the college class which she taught, hundreds of young men were challenged to go into the ministry. Furthermore, the Gospel Light Sunday School literature written by Dr. Mears and her co-workers at the Hollywood church eventually became the material that now circles the globe.

But this outstanding and fruitful life was not without a period of crisis in her younger days. She had many male friends but really loved only one, a man of a different faith. When faced with tension and conflict about this decision she turned to the Lord and prayed: "Lord, You have made me the way I am. I love a home, I love security, I love children, and I love him. Yet I feel that marriage under these conditions would draw me away from You. I surrender even this, Lord, and leave it in Your hands. Lead me, Lord, and strengthen me. You have promised to fulfill all my needs. I trust in You alone."[2]

After this prayer the friendship was ended. Many years later as she looked back on this experience, Dr. Mears wrote: "The marvelous thing has been that the Lord has always given me a beautiful home; He has given me thousands of children; He has supplied every need in my life, and I've never felt lonely. Since I am a very gregarious person, I thought I would have a feeling I didn't belong. But I've never had it, never! I've never missed companionship. Through one experience after another the Lord has shown me that He had something special for me to do. After I went through that final door, where it was just the Lord and I, into wide open spaces of people and things and excitement, life has been one great adventure."[3]

This does not mean that every single Christian girl need experience the success of Dr. Mears. Quantity is not the key; rather, it's quality. A human being can discover fulfillment in many fulfilling relationships or just a few. The important thing is that a single girl must somehow break the shackles of a cultural conditioning that tells her the only route to happiness is marriage (or some other form of sexual intimacy with the opposite sex).

Though God ordained marriage and family life as a major means for fulfillment, it is not the only way. There are other avenues available for the woman who gains a proper perspective on life and eternal values. Most important, she must realize that Jesus Christ is her constant companion. Furthermore, being a member of a loving, functioning Body of Christ can provide rich and fulfilling relationships.

Question for Discussion: How would you counsel an older single girl who is terribly frustrated about her single state?

Step B: As a married woman, evaluate your marital and family life-style in the light of Paul's injunction to "be busy at home." Have you established proper priorities? Are you so busy *outside* the home that you are neglecting the needs of your husband and children? The following checklist will help you make proper judgments.

Because of my busy schedule:

☐ I am too tired to cook meals and keep the house in order.

☐ I am increasingly losing interest in my home.

☐ I feel under constant pressure, never having enough time to do what needs to be done.

☐ My husband is showing signs of stress and anxiety because of my inability to get things done on time.

☐ I have very little time to entertain in the home and show hospitality.

☐ I become irritated with the children because I'm tired.

☐ I want to eat out all the time.

Note: All of these symptoms can be present without the stress of outside activity. What might cause these problems in a woman who is not overly active outside the home? What suggestions do you have to help her overcome her problems?

Footnotes

1. Billy Graham, Introduction to *The Henrietta Mears Story,* by Barbara Hudson Powers (Westwood, NJ: Revell, 1957), p. 7.
2. Ethel M. Baldwin and David V. Benson, *Henrietta Mears and How She Did It* (Ventura, California: Gospel Light, Regal Books, 1966), pp. 42-43.
3. *Henrietta Mears and How She Did It,* p. 43.

12 TO BE KIND

"Likewise, teach the older women . . . then they can train the younger women . . . to be kind." (Titus 2:3-5)

In Joppa there was a disciple named Tabitha (which means Dorcas), who was always *doing good* and *helping the poor.* She became sick and died. Her body was washed and placed in an upstairs room. Other disciples in Joppa heard that Peter was in Lydda, not far from Joppa. So they sent two men to him and urged him, "Please come at once!"

"Peter went with them, and when he arrived he was taken upstairs to the room. All the widows stood around him, crying and *showing him the robes and other clothing* that Dorcas had made while she was still with them" (Acts 9:39).

What began as a very sad story ended with great excitement and rejoicing and conversions to Jesus Christ. Peter, in the power of the Holy Spirit, raised Dorcas from the dead, and consequently "many people believed in the Lord" (Acts 9:36-43).

The primary reason Luke recorded this miracle in the

book of Acts is because "many people believed in the Lord." Miracles were basically designed by God to confirm the message of salvation (see Heb. 2:2-4). But there is another important truth that stands out in bold relief in this story: Dorcas was a "good" woman, a woman who illustrates quite graphically what Paul had in mind when he instructed older women to teach the younger women to be "kind" (see Titus 2:3-5).

Actually, most Bible translators use the word "good" to express in English what Paul meant in the language of his day. And Luke tells us Dorcas was *always* "doing good."

The basic Greek word, *agathos,* that Luke used to describe Dorcas and Paul used to describe a mature Christian woman, means to excel in any respect, to be distinguished, to be *good.*

Agathos, in the New Testament, describes not only people, but things, conditions, deeds, times and seasons. When it is used to describe people, the word is sometimes used in a narrower sense—a person who is benevolent, kind, or generous. This explains why the translators of the *New International Version* use the word "kind" to convey the meaning of *agathos.*

No doubt Dorcas stands out in Scripture as a unique illustration of the kind of woman Paul was describing. Her good deeds involved "helping the poor," and later in the same passage we are told exactly how she did this. The widows who gathered to mourn her death held in their hands the *"robes* and other *clothes"* Dorcas made while she was still with them. She was a kind and generous woman who used her sewing skills to meet the needs of others.

A First-Century Meaning

In his first letter to Timothy Paul describes what he had in mind when he instructed older women to teach younger women to be good or kind. In this correspondence he was dealing with widows who were *truly* widows; that is, they had no children or grandchildren to help care for their daily needs. The apostle proceeded to set forth a specific criteria for evaluating a woman who was eligible for material assistance. "No widow" wrote Paul, "may be put on the list of widows [that is, to be cared for by the church] unless she is over sixty, has been faithful to her husband, and is well-known for her good deeds, such as bringing up children, showing hospitality, washing the feet of the saints, helping those in trouble and devoting herself to all kinds of good deeds" (1 Tim. 5:9,10).

First, Paul indicated that this kind of woman must be over 60 years old; that is, beyond the age when the average widow would consider remarriage and also beyond the age when she could ordinarily care for her own needs.

Second, she must be a woman who has been morally pure; that is, faithful to her husband.

And thirdly, she must be "well-known for her *good deeds.*" And at this point Paul leaves no room for speculation regarding what he had in mind. He spelled out specific things that were to be considered *"good deeds."*

A Description of Good Deeds

At the top of Paul's list is "bringing up children." What kind of mother was she? Was she faithful? Did she consider this her primary responsibility in the home?

Note: This criteria provides a much needed balance when describing doing "good deeds." Some Christians are so busy meeting the needs of others that they neglect their own children. To make sure this didn't happen, and before he described other good deeds, Paul specified that "bringing up children" should be a priority.

Next Paul speaks of "showing hospitality." How has this woman used her home? Has she shared it with others?

Has she been unselfish with her own material blessings?

In Scripture, "hospitality" is often listed as a Christian duty (see Rom. 12:13; Heb. 13:1,2; 1 Pet. 4:9). When specifying the qualifications for Christian leadership in the church, Paul twice mentioned "hospitality" as a mark of Christian maturity (see 1 Tim. 3:2; Titus 1:8). And, as just noted, "hospitality" is also considered as a sign of a "good" woman. To paraphrase Paul more specifically, "older women were to teach the younger women to be hospitable."

Third in the "good deeds" list is "washing the feet of the saints." In Bible times, people gave special attention to their feet and the feet of others. Open sandals on dusty roads created obvious difficulties. Consequently, it was a common practice for a host to wash a visitor's feet, which became a means of showing hospitality and of demonstrating humility. (Jesus Christ made this point dramatically when He stopped to wash His disciples' feet in John 13:4-15.) Paul classified washing feet as a "good deed."

Fourth, Paul said good deeds is helping "those in trouble." This, of course, is an "open-ended" idea. Helping those in trouble might include any kind of difficulty and involve almost any kind of assistance. It might range from sharing a cup of cold water to being a good Samaritan.

Paul concluded his list with "devoting yourself to all kinds of good deeds."[1] This statement is merely an extension of the open-ended idea just stated. With this remark Paul was demonstrating that what he had just listed as "good deeds" were merely introductory comments that illustrated what could be done. And necessarily so!

What may have been good deeds in one situation may not have been relevant in another. And furthermore, what may have been a good deed in the first-century culture may no longer be necessary in our twentieth-century culture—such as washing the feet of saints. But in every culture, there are many ways to be devoted to doing "all kinds of good deeds." And Paul certainly implied that a woman who is maturing in her Christian faith will be the kind of woman who does good deeds.

A Personal or Group Project

The following personal project is designed to help you become, to a greater degree, a Christian woman who is classified as being kind and good.

Step A: Note the following Scriptures that reinforce the importance of "doing good" in order to be in the will of God:

1. We are to do *good* to all people—Christians and non-Christians.

• "Let us not become weary in *doing good*, for at the proper time we will reap a harvest if we do not give up. Therefore, as we have opportunity, let us *do good* to all people, especially to those who belong to the family of believers" (Gal. 6:9,10).

• "Remind the people to be subject to rulers and authorities, to be obedient, to be ready *to do whatever is good*, to slander no one, to be peaceable and considerate, and to show true humility toward all men" (Titus 3:1,2).

2. Doing good should be a natural result of our salvation.

• "For it is by grace you have been saved, through faith—and this not from yourselves, it is the gift of God—not by works, so that no one can boast. For we are God's workmanship, created in Christ Jesus *to do good works*, which God prepared in advance for us to do" (Eph. 2:8-10).

3. Doing good involves what we *say* as well as what we do.

• "Do not let any unwholesome talk come out of your mouths, but only what is helpful [good] for building others up according to their needs, that it may benefit those who listen" (Eph. 4:29).

4. Employee/employer relationships help give us unique opportunities to do good.

• "Slaves, obey your earthly masters with respect and fear, and with sincerity of heart, just as you would obey Christ . . . . Serve wholeheartedly, as if you were serving the Lord, not men, because you know that the Lord will reward everyone for whatever *good* he does, whether he is slave or free" (Eph. 6:5,7,8).

5. Our prayer, like Paul's, should be that we will bear fruit in every good work.

• "And we pray this in order that you may live a life worthy of the Lord and may please Him in every way: *bearing fruit in every good work,* growing in the knowledge of God" (Col. 1:10).

6. A Christian should avoid returning evil for evil.

• "Make sure that nobody pays back wrong for wrong, but always try to be kind [good] to each other and to everyone else" (1 Thess. 5:15).

• "Do not repay evil with evil or insult with insult, but with blessing, because to this you were called so that you may inherit a blessing . . . . He must turn from evil and do *good;* he must seek peace and pursue it" (1 Pet. 3:9,11).

Step B: Using Paul's list of good deeds in 1 Timothy 5:10 as a model, make up a list of good deeds that would be uniquely twentieth-century, and within the particular culture in with you live. Be specific!

Step C: Now that you have completed the list, indicate which ones you feel are priority items in the life of the average person. Also, note any cautions that must be taken in doing these things.

Step D: Now that you have a clear perspective on what it means to "be kind or good," set up a realistic schedule for applying these truths in your own life. For example, a minimal goal within the range of most people is to select one person per week for the next month and determine what you are going to do for that person.

Remember: In some instances, words are as effective as deeds in doing good, especially as a means of encouragement and comfort. However, in some instances words can never replace deeds. At this point we must remember the words of James, who said: "Suppose a brother or sister is without clothes and daily food. If one of you *says* to him, 'Go, I wish you well; keep warm and fed.' but does nothing about his physical needs, what good is it?" (Jas. 2:15,16).

Footnotes

1. There are two words used in the New Testament which are frequently translated "good." In Titus 2:5, Paul used the word *agathos*. In 1 Timothy 5:10, when describing "good deeds," Paul first used the word *kalos* and then ended the verse with the word *agathos*. Both words are used dozens of times in the New Testament to describe basically the same concept, "doing good" as contrasted with "doing evil."

13 TO BE SUBJECT TO THEIR HUSBANDS

"The older women can train the younger women . . . to be subject to their husbands." (Titus 2:3-5)

The subject of submission, like Paul's injunction "to be busy at home," has emerged in the twentieth century as very controversial among both men and women, Christians and non-Christians. Among some believers it is emphasized and reemphasized in numerous seminars across the country. Articles and books on the subject have multiplied.

Interestingly, many of those who bear down hardest on the importance of submission are women.

More recently, a number of Christians, both men and women, raised serious questions about his emphasis, claiming that what is often taught misrepresents the true teaching of Scripture. Personally, I would have to align myself with those who raise these questions. Often the subject is treated without sufficient explanations and qualifications. However, the Bible does teach submission.

It seems Christians often misunderstand and misinterpret biblical writers; Paul particularly, because he wrote more on the subject of submission than other writers did. Some of this misunderstanding is the result of inadequate interpretation—taking statements out of context, misunderstanding what is cultural and supracultural, or sometimes superimposing present-day twentieth-century forms upon biblical functions. But, and in a much more limited sense, some Christians make the Bible teach what they want it to teach, reflecting their own subjectivity, bias and prejudice—something all of us must be on guard against as we study and interpret Scripture.

But whatever the cause of the misunderstanding, some people are led to an erroneous view of what Paul meant when he wrote to Titus, "Teach the older women to . . . train the younger women . . . to *be subject to their husbands.*"

What *did* Paul mean in this passage as well as in other similar passages? To the Ephesians and Colossians he said, without equivocation, "Wives, *submit* to your husbands" (Eph. 5:22; Col. 3:18). And to make sure the Ephesian Christians really understood what he said, he added, "Now as the church *submits* to Christ, so also wives should submit to their husbands in *everything*" (Eph. 5:24).

Peter, too, emphasized the same kind of behavior, particularly toward their non-Christian husbands. "Wives," he said, "in the same way be *submissive* to your husbands so that, if any of them do not believe the Word, they may be won over without talk by the behavior of their wives" (1 Pet. 3:1).

What Submission Is Not

Wives were not the only ones who were to practice submission. Paul, before exhorting wives to submit to their husbands (see Eph. 5:22), exhorted *all* believers to "submit to one another out of reverence for Christ" (Eph. 5:21). All members of the Body of Christ were to practice submission, including wives to husbands and husbands to wives.

Paul extended this concept of mutual submission to the intimacies of marriage when he wrote to the Corinthians: "The husband should fulfill his marital duty to his wife, and likewise the wife to her husband. The wife's body does not belong to her alone but also to her husband. In the same way, the husband's body does not belong to him alone but also to his wife. Do not deprive each other except by mutual consent and for a time, so that you may devote yourselves to prayer. Then come together again so that Satan will not tempt you because of your lack of self-control" (1 Cor. 7:3-5).

Submission does not mean wives should never express their opinions or feelings. Some Christian men refuse to let their wives express feelings and frustrations, anxieties and anger. Any disagreement is put down with the "authority" of Scripture.

Nothing could be more biblically inaccurate or devastating to a woman's self-worth and emotional and spiritual health.

To deny their wives this privilege is a direct violation of Peter's exhortation to husbands to treat their wives "with respect" and "as heirs in Christ Jesus." Such husbands are not loving as Christ loved. They are in direct violation of many biblical injunctions that exhort all Christians (which certainly includes husbands and wives) to "be devoted to one another" (Rom. 12:10), to "accept one another" (Rom. 15:7), to "serve one another" (Gal. 5:13), to "carry each other's burdens" (Gal. 6:2), and to "encourage each other" (1 Thess. 4:18). Paul made it very clear in his Corinthian letter that all Christians are to have "equal concern for each other." And then he added: "If one part suffers every part suffers with it" (1 Cor. 12:25,26).

The Christian husband who is not sensitive to his wife, who does not listen to her complaints, who does not identify with her emotional and physical pain, is in direct violation of God's will. He is no doubt using the Scriptures to justify his own weak ego and his selfish and egotistical behavior.

There are some men, even Christian men, who use the concept of headship to justify authoritarian attitudes and behavior in marriage. They try to run their homes like an army sergeant. They shout orders, demand instant obedience to every whim and wish, and meet opposition with psychological, if not physical, force. This is not "headship!" It's childishness and selfishness. It is the opposite of "love."

True, God has given man a position of headship in the home (Eph. 5:23). But this does not guarantee that his wife (or his children) will automatically respect and honor him from her heart. If a woman tries to recognize her husband's position of authority in her life she will have difficulty following through at the "feeling" level if he does not, as Peter exhorted, treat her "with respect" (1 Pet. 3:7). Respect begets respect. Practically speaking, it is earned, even though God gives man the position. How man handles this sacred trust determines to a great extent whether or not he will indeed be the respected head of the household.

Furthermore, the Bible does not teach that man should be the sole decision-maker in the home. Although the concept of headship certainly involves authority, it does not imply that the wife is incapable of making decisions, nor does it mean she should not be significantly involved in the process.

Submission does not mean a wife should indulge in sin

because her husband demands it. When Paul stated that wives should "submit to their husbands in *everything*," he certainly did not mean they should violate God's revealed will. Again, there are obvious teachings in Scripture that help us interpret what Paul meant. There are times when Christian wives must say, just as Peter and the apostles did in Jerusalem, I must "obey God rather than men" (Acts 5:29).

But a word of warning. A Christian wife, before she resists her husband's demands, must be sure that what he wants her to do is indeed a violation of God's revealed will. It is very easy for a person to justify resistance on the basis of predetermined notions and convictions that are not based on Scripture but rather on tradition and culture.

Submission does not mean a wife must subject herself to physical and psychological abuse that is beyond her ability to bear. Unfortunately, some women are married to men who are so self-centered and evil in their actions that it is impossible to cope with the problems. No matter what she does to try to be a submissive wife, he only takes greater advantage. A man like this is sick, spiritually and psychologically. At this point a Christian wife needs to seek help and advice from the elders and pastors of her local church. She cannot bear the problem alone. This is a matter for church discipline (Matt. 18:15-17; Jas. 5:13-26). In times like this, a woman needs help from other mature members of the Body of Christ who can help her confront her husband with his sins.

But again a word of warning! Some women find it very easy to rationalize and project themselves as unappreciated martyrs, but in reality they have not been obedient to Scripture. They have defined submissiveness by their own standards, not by the Word of God.

But this leads us once again to the basic question: What *do* the writers of Scripture mean by submission?

What Submission Is

Submission refers to an attitude of "teachableness" toward other members of the Body of Christ. Teachableness includes a willingness to yield to another person's advice or admonition. When necessary, it means being willing to submit to another person's control.

As we said earlier, submission is an attitude every Christian should have toward all members of Christ's body.

What the Bible says to all Christians generally, regarding their relationships with one another, also applies to Christian husbands and wives specifically. But since the family is a specialized unit, often surfacing specific problems that are uniquely different from a local body of believers, the Bible goes a step further and gives some special instructions to husbands and wives, as well as parents and children. Some of these instructions, as we'll see later, *were* directly related to cultural conditions in the New Testament world. But the cultural conditions calling for certain *emphases* by Paul and Peter in no way eliminate the supracultural principle of wifely submission. This concept permeates the whole of Scripture.

God created woman for man. The authority for statements made by New Testament writers regarding submission are rooted and grounded in the creation story. After God created Adam, He said: "It is not good for the man to be alone; I will make him a helper suitable for him" (Gen. 2:18, *NASB*). Following through on Adam's deep social need, the Lord "caused a deep sleep to fall upon the man, and he slept; then He took one of his ribs, and closed up the flesh at that place. And the Lord God fashioned into a woman the rib which He had taken from the man, and brought her *to the man*" (Gen. 2:21,22, *NASB*).

Many years later, when the apostle Paul was discussing the subject of worship with the Corinthian Christians, he argued a point based upon the same biblical truth from the creation story. Said he: "For man did not come from woman, *but woman from man;* neither was man created for woman, *but woman for man*" (1 Cor. 11:8,9).

Here Paul was referring to God's order in creation as well as His purpose in creating woman. What Paul is referring to happened before sin came into the world. In other words, the fall affected woman's present relation to man, but before the fall, in God's original plan He created woman *for man* and thus determined woman's relationship *to man.* In the same Corinthian letter, Paul made this truth even stronger when he emphasized that man is "the image and *glory of God;* but the woman is the *glory of man*" (1 Cor. 11:7).

By creation, man first reflected God's unique image; and since woman was taken from man, she, in a special way, reflected the unique image of man. Although certainly it follows that she also reflected the image of God.

As we've already seen, the apostle Peter also affirms this same concept (see 1 Pet. 3:1-6). It hardly seems feasible to interpret these passages, explaining submission and divine order in both the Old and New Testaments, as purely cultural statements. The whole tone of Scripture teaches that man, by creation, has a position of authority in the family.

Woman's role was complicated by the fall. It is very important to understand that woman's relationship with man was severely affected by the entrance of sin into the human race. After Eve first disobeyed God and Adam followed her example, God clearly referred to the effect of sin upon her relationship to her husband. To Eve God said: "I will greatly multiply your pain in childbirth, in pain you shall bring forth children; yet your desire shall be for your husband, and he shall rule over you" (Gen. 3:16, *NASB*).

Woman's submissive role to man, then, *antedates* the fall, but was *complicated* by the fall. Once sin entered the human race, it set up all kinds of problems in the relationship between man and woman, one being that man too became a sinner, causing him to abuse and misuse his God-ordained role as head of the household. And unfortunately, many women have suffered ever since.

Men have been notorious throughout history for using women for their own ends. On the current scene we see the Playboy philosophy that views women as toys, playthings, as a means to selfish pleasure. It is no wonder that most thinking women react against this self-centered philosophy. Today, more than ever before, women are used for materialistic business purposes. Sex sells anything, and women of course are the primary targets for this abuse. Again, it should not be surprising that thinking women would react to such selfish endeavors.

Women are reacting to the general male selfishness that permeates the whole society in which we live. Women are often treated as inferior personalities, incapable of certain roles. They are often "kept in their place" because men are threatened by their abilities. It should not surprise us that mature women (and even immature women) can see through such egocentric behavior.

Where can these women turn? Where is their source of authority for what they do? Unfortunately, most do not have, or else they reject, the divine perspective. Since they do not know Christ, we should be able to understand their reactive behavior. Motivated by the same sinful nature that motivates men, they are seeking liberation without God's principles. And, of course, they do not realize that without Jesus Christ they can never know true freedom. Consequently, they react, first in one direction and then another. It is no wonder that the world is filled with frustrated people, many sincerely trying, but never able to come to a knowledge of God's ways and the secret to what they are looking for.

Christians too are to blame. All too many Bible students use the Scriptures to teach submission in a way that violates the very nature of women. This approach, along with what the world generally does, causes many sincere and perceptive Christians to attempt to harmonize Christianity with current trends by teaching that biblical writers were also in error. Rather than exposing erroneous interpretations of Scripture, they compromise their position on biblical authority. This is unfortunate indeed.

Cultural or Supracultural?

As we stated in an earlier chapter, we do not believe that what Paul and other biblical writers taught on the subject of submission reflects cultural hangovers from their Jewish backgrounds. Though we certainly would not deny the influence of culture, these writers were inspired by the Holy Spirit and what they wrote is applicable to all time. It is a supracultural principle.

In trying to determine what in the Scriptures is cultural and what is supracultural, what is nonabsolute and what is absolute, *consistency* is a very important factor. If the New Testament writers extend their concept of submission to include relationships between men and women in the church (and they do), then it doesn't seem proper to treat submission as a cultural concept.[1]

It is necessary, however, for us to know some cultural factors that existed in the New Testament world before we can adequately interpret passages in the New Testament that have to do with submission. Perhaps the most significant cultural factor was the attitude authority figures in general had toward others. The New Testament writers dealt with this in writing to slaves who became Christians. In the twentieth-century world of business the New Testament principle that we are to submit to those in authority over us, is certainly applicable. But it was even *more* applicable in the first century. For a slave to demand his freedom after he became a Christian could easily have resulted in severe physical punishment and even death for him. Thus Peter wrote: "Slaves, submit yourselves to your masters with all respect, not only to those who are good and considerate but also to those who are harsh" (1 Pet. 2:18; see also Eph. 6:5; Col. 3:22).

The apostles took the same approach in relationship to government. Paul wrote, "Everyone must submit himself to the governing authorities" (Rom. 13:1). And for what purpose? Because it is the right thing to do; not only that but Paul adds, "Do you want to be free from fear of the one in authority? Then do what is right and he will commend you" (Rom. 13:3; see also 1 Pet. 2:18). In other words, there is a personal benefit from submitting oneself to the government: freedom from fear.

For this same reason Paul said, without equivocation, "Wives, submit to your husbands" (Eph. 5:22; Col. 3:18); Peter included an added benefit: "Wives . . . be submissive to your husbands so that, if any of them do not believe the Word, they may be won over without talk by the behavior of their wives" (1 Pet. 3:1). A cultural factor in the first-century world was one of the hostile environment. Women were particularly victims of their culture because, in some instances, they are considered very dispensable. Their harsh and insensitive husbands could quickly dispose of them and replace them with someone else.

The approach, then, that both Paul and Peter took to help penetrate the cultural barriers of that day in government, in business and in marriage, was to *emphasize* submission. For though the principle of submission, particularly in marriage, was established by God from the beginning, at Creation, and again after the fall, the principle had special meaning for New Testament believers because it was a key to emotional and, in some cases, physical survival. Furthermore, it became a dynamic means to win husbands to Jesus Christ. This is why Peter bore down hard on this subject in his first epistle (see 1 Pet. 3:1-6). Interestingly, we see the same evangelism purpose in relationships to government leaders and pagan slave owners (see 1 Tim. 2:1-4; Titus 2:9,10).

Spiritual Equality

There is yet another perspective on the concept of submission in the New Testament.

When sin entered the world it brought with it some special difficulties for all people, but especially for women (see Gen. 3:16). Though this may appear to some as unfair and unjust, we can only accept the fact that it is a reality. God is righteous and just, and as His creatures, we must submit to Him in all that He is and does. Of course, the greatest thing He ever did for this world was to send His Son, Jesus Christ, to deal with the problem of sin.

By the death and resurrection of Jesus Christ, God gave men and women (especially husbands and wives) a new opportunity for oneness and equality. In Christ, wrote Paul, "There is neither Jew nor Greek, slave nor free, *male nor female,* for you are all one in Christ Jesus" (Gal. 3:26-28).

Here Paul is dealing with our spiritual *position* as Christians. In God's sight we are all one. In fact, we're already glorified (see Rom. 8:29,30). From God's viewpoint we are already in heaven. This is why Jesus Christ stated that there will be no marriage in heaven. Sex distinctions are eliminated.

But the Bible also recognizes the fact that, practically speaking, we're still involved in the process. We are still victims of space and time, and, though we are free from the power of sin, it is still present in the world and is still operative in our hearts, even as Christians. For example, in this same passage, Paul wrote there is neither "slave nor free" from the perspective of eternity, yet the Bible clearly recognizes that a slave in the New Testament world was not yet free from the effects of sin. The same is true of all human beings in all human relationships, including marriage.

The challenge of the New Testament is day by day to become more and more like Jesus Christ, until we are no longer in process but with Him in glory. And when it comes to marriage, in Christ there is a certain restoration with great potential. A Christian husband and wife have the opportunity to experience a unity and oneness that can grow constantly deeper and more meaningful day by day. Spiritually, there is once again total equality. But functionally, man is still recognized as the head, and the woman is to submit to his authority. Sin has not yet been eradicated. But in Christ if a husband and wife continually and regularly fulfill their God-ordained roles, they have the potential to experience a foretaste of heaven on this side of glory.

This, of course, represents the ideal. But because of sin, Paul had to exhort husbands to love their wives as Christ loved the church (see Eph. 5:25). And he had to exhort wives to submit as the church is to submit to Christ (see Eph. 5:22-24). But for those who take the Word of God seriously, there is little need to continually repeat these exhortations. In fact, couples can actually experience on a day to day basis oneness and unity that leads to consensus and egalitarian benefits.

Let me add a personal illustration. Though marriage for my wife and I has certainly had its share of difficulties, we have attempted to obey God in these matters. And upon reflection, we can think of only one occasion when I had to overrule my wife in a decision. In all other significant decisions we have come to a consensus through a process of mutual discussion and interaction. Furthermore, I have never, to my knowledge, ever viewed my wife as an inferior person.

Ironically, on the occasion when I did overrule Elaine, I can see now that if I had been more perceptive and sensitive, in short spiritually and psychologically mature, I would not have had to make the decision I did. If I had it to do over again, I would accept her feelings in the matter. But this only illustrates, of course, why God had to lay down these regulations. We are still not glorified and even though we are attempting to live for Jesus Christ, there are times when our old nature gets in the way. And I must also add that after years of marriage counseling, I have observed that not all married women are as sensitive as my wife in desiring to do the will of God.

A Personal or Group Project

The following personal project is designed to help you evaluate your personal situation as a wife (or if single, your future situation), and to be able to obey the biblical injunction to be submissive, and yet to understand the total context of scriptural teaching regarding this matter. The following case studies will help you gain insight.

Jane is married to a Christian man and she feels he is unreasonable in his demands regarding keeping up the house. She believes he is unrealistic regarding neatness, especially since they have small children. She feels she has tried hard to please her husband but he is never satisfied. He rides her constantly about the matter and she is developing deep feelings of resentment. How would you advise Jane in this matter?

Diane is frustrated with the sexual part of her marriage. She reports that her husband's sexual demands are too great. For her, submission has not solved the problem.

She reports that the more she is available, the more demands he puts on her. Consequently, she is becoming angry and resentful. She admits that she now withdraws and avoids the situation—which makes matters worse. How would you advise Diane?

Mary reports that her husband is highly threatened by any kind of dialogue and discussion. If she expresses her opinion, he feels she is not being submissive. Consequently, she is harboring some deep feelings of resentment. How would you advise Mary to resolve that problem?

Note: Write out several other case studies that reflect realistic situations and discuss their possible solutions in the light of the biblical perspective just presented.

Footnote

1. For further treatment of this concept, see Gene A. Getz, *The Measure of a Family* (Ventura, Calif.: Regal Books, 1977), ch. 3.

14 A
GENTLE
AND QUIET SPIRIT

"Your beauty should not come from outward adornment, such as braided hair and the wearing of gold jewelry and fine clothes. Instead, it should be that of your inner self, the unfading beauty of a gentle and quiet spirit, which is of great worth in God's sight." (1 Pet. 3:3,4)

The general trend of culture from time immemorial has always run counter to the apostle Peter's description of a beautiful woman in 1 Peter 3:3,4. Should you doubt this observation, the backdrop of the present American society serves as a vivid illustration and reminder of this reality. To be popular and attractive today, a woman must be "sexy" and "sensual." And our twentieth-century media techniques are uniquely designed to exploit this mania, particularly in the field of advertising. A woman's physical attributes are used to sell most everything.

In this particular passage of Scripture, Peter emphasized "purity" and "reverence" among women as a mark of beauty and attractiveness (1 Pet. 3:2). Our present society emphasizes impurity and irreverence. Peter also emphasized "inner qualities" as a mark of attractiveness and real beauty (1 Pet. 3:4). Our modern society emphasizes external qualities. Finally, Peter emphasized a "gentle and quiet spirit," whereas the modern liberation movement particularly advocates the opposite.

External Beauty

At this juncture it is important to clarify one very significant point. External beauty per se is not sinful. In fact, God created "woman for man" (1 Cor. 11:9). As mentioned in the very beginning of this book, God uniquely designed woman to be sexually attractive. Furthermore, God certainly is not opposed to women making themselves externally beautiful. To conclude from this passage of Scripture in Peter's epistle, as some Christians do, that in itself is wrong to wear jewelry, that it is worldly and sinful for a woman to fix her hair attractively and to wear beautiful clothes is to miss the whole point.

What the Scriptures *are* teaching, particularly in this passage, is that there is something far more basic to external beauty in attracting and impressing men, even unsaved husbands. This is why Peter wrote, "wives, . . . be submissive to your husbands so that, if any of them do not believe the word, they may be won over without talk by the behavior of their wives." Then Peter states *how* this can be done: "When they see the *purity and reverence* of your lives" (1 Pet. 3:1,2).

Among other things, Peter is dealing with the concept of sexual purity in this passage, which he closely correlates with his emphasis on internal beauty, a "gentle and quiet spirit." No doubt many of these New Testament Christian women found it easy to slip back into some of their old pagan habits of trying to attract men other than their legal husbands by means of external beauty, "outward adornment, such as braided hair and the wearing of gold jewelry and fine clothes" (v. 3). This became the means to an immoral end.

But there is also a significant point here for Christian women who *are* faithful to their husbands. External beauty *is* important to a man. It is not wrong to use it as a means of pleasing the man you truly love and are committed to in a legal marriage. (For abundance of evidence for this fact read the Song of Solomon.)

But the fact remains that physical beauty alone will never endure as a means of pleasing a husband. In fact, without inner beauty, which Peter defines as a "gentle and quiet spirit," external beauty quickly becomes superficial. It may achieve certain goals for a brief time in the bedroom, but it is inner beauty that attracts and endures and wins respect over the years. Furthermore, it is inner beauty that makes external qualities even more attractive.

Gentleness

As with submission and purity, "a gentle and quiet spirit" is not exclusively required of women, particularly the characteristic of "gentleness." In fact, Jesus, one day as He taught the crowds on the mountainside, enumerated a number of Christian qualities. Among them was *gentleness*. "Blessed are the meek [the gentle]," He explained, "for they will inherit the earth" (Matt. 5:5). Jesus exemplified this quality in His own life when He fulfilled an Old Testament prophecy and rode into Jerusalem astride a donkey. "See, your king comes to you," proclaimed the prophet Zechariah, "*gentle* and riding on a donkey" (Matt. 21:5). That day the Lord of the universe appeared as the "gentle Jesus."

Paul particularly exhorted all Christians to exemplify this quality in their lives. He designated "gentleness" as reflecting the fruit of the Spirit (see Gal. 5:22,23). To the

Ephesian Christians, he wrote: "Be completely humble and *gentle*" (Eph. 4:2). Likewise, he exhorted the Colossians to clothe themselves with "gentleness" (Col. 3:12). Twice Paul encouraged Timothy to always be gentle. Pursue it, wrote Paul in his first letter (see 1 Tim. 6:11), and even when Timothy faced those who opposed him, he was to "*gently* instruct," trusting that God would give them a change of heart "leading them to a knowledge of the truth" (2 Tim. 2:25).

There is no question that gentleness is a mark of Christian maturity for *all* Christians and in *all* relationships. But in a special sense it is a quality for Christian women, especially as it is associated with the related quality of "quietness." Furthermore, "quietness" among women is frequently associated in Scripture with the quality of submission, not only in the passage in Peter's epistle where he uses the word "submission" twice (see 1 Pet. 3:1,5), but also in the writings of Paul (see 1 Cor. 14:34; 1 Tim. 2:11). Communication per se is not the basic issue in the Scriptures on being quiet. Rather "quietness" or "silence," as it is often translated, refers to the "spirit" in which a woman communicates. Peter called this a "gentle spirit," a "quiet spirit." Personally, I believe "quietness" is related to her very God-created nature and, in turn, appeals to the God-created nature in man. When she violates this principle it causes a negative reaction from the average man and, interestingly, other women. In fact, some women react more negatively against a loud and boisterous woman than do some men.

On occasions we've all seen women violate this biblical principle in a public situation. In one instance, a husband and his wife were making application for their license plates. As usual, people by the scores were lined up waiting. For some reason this couple was having difficulty securing legal permission for some particular need. Suddenly, the woman burst forth with volley of vulgar oaths that would have made an old sea captain blush. Everyone in the place could hear and see what was happening. The husband, literally and spontaneously and without premeditation, looked for a place to hide. Unfortunately, there wasn't any. If he could have found a hole in the floor he would have, without hesitation, dropped out of sight. It was really a rather pathetic scene.

On another occasion, we were watching a little league football game in which our son was participating. The opposing team (which was losing) was coached by a woman who didn't hesitate to let her little charges know what she thought of their inadequate performance.

As my wife and I stood on the sidelines with the parents of both teams and watched and *listened,* a very interesting phenomenon unfolded before our eyes. One by one, the parents of our team, including us, began to move to the other side of the field. We can only speculate *why* this happened. They must have been "feeling" the same emotional reactions we were—embarrassed for her, the boys, and their parents.

Elaine and I have reflected on this experience in conjunction with the subject of this chapter, "a gentle and quiet spirit." Our conclusion is that the main issue or the problem was not that a woman was coaching a football team. Rather, it was her tone of voice, her attitude, her communication techniques. And within us, and many others, welled up negative emotions and reactions.

We realize, of course, that some people would classify our conclusion as being culturally conditioned, and we immediately acknowledge this is probably true to a certain extent. However, we believe it is more than that. We believe our feelings relate to a God-created difference in men and women. People are naturally attracted to a "gentle and quiet spirit" in a woman, and embarrassed, in some instances repulsed, by a loud and unfeminine demonstration.

True, a loud, boisterous and insensitive man is also repulsive. But a woman more so. Thus the apostle Peter exhorts women to demonstrate a "gentle and quiet spirit," thereby showing internal beauty that is attractive to others, particularly to non-Christian husbands.

To demonstrate the supracultural nature of these qualities, Peter illustrated his point by referring to "the way the holy women of the past . . . used to make themselves beautiful." Specifically, the apostle mentioned Sarah, Abraham's wife, who exemplified submission with her purity, her reverence, and her gentle and quiet spirit (1 Pet. 3:5,6).

A Personal or Group Project
Step A: Run a check on yourself to determine how you sound to others. Following are some suggestions.

1. If married, ask your husband and children to give you feedback. If single, ask some of your closest friends. Be specific. Ask them to honestly tell you how you sound in certain situations:

When you want something done around the house;

When a meal is ready to be served;

When you are frustrated and angry;

When you are tired;

Other:

Note: This is a threatening experience. But if you follow through as objectively as possible, you'll discover information that will help you to become a more mature and godly woman.

Remember: You cannot change something unless you know exactly what bothers others.

2. If the previous suggestion creates too much anxi-

ety, begin the process by evaluating yourself. You might set up a small tape recorder in the vicinity of your regular activities. During certain times when you face the most stress and frustration, turn it on and record your reactions. Later on, listen to see how you sound.

Note: Knowing you are recording your own voice will motivate you to be more composed. Try to ignore this tendency and react as you normally do. Try to forget that the tape recorder is going.

Remember: This alternative suggestion is not the most effective method you can use. It involves too many subjective variables. However, it's a good stepping stone to direct communication. Use it as a "means" to another "end": to interact with and gain feedback from those who are closest to you.

Step B: Once you gain sufficient data to evaluate the ways others "see" and "hear" you, isolate your most vulnerable moments. Are there any observable patterns? Is it when you are tired? When you are under undue pressure? A certain time of the month? At mealtime? Et cetera.

Note: Some people develop bad vocal habits. For example, a woman who was reared in a home where her mother was loud and boisterous tends to develop the same vocal qualities. This *can* be changed, but it takes conscious and persistent effort. Note, too, that a woman's voice can be far more shrill, cutting, and irritating than a man's, simply because of the innate pitch. A woman naturally speaks an octave higher than a man, which makes her more vulnerable to unpleasant communication.

Step C: If necessary, outline a program for change. For example, the following suggestions will help you:

1. If there are noticeable periods of time when you violate Peter's principle, attempt to be on guard ahead of time.

2. If married, ask your husband and children to help

you accomplish your goals. Ask for their understanding and prayers.

3. Consciously attempt to view frustrating situations as opportunities to maintain control of your communication. How you perceive the situation often helps you to avoid slipping into certain habitual reactions.

4. If your vocal qualities are a result of learning and bad habits, seek help from a speech specialist, someone who can work with you and give you some helpful suggestions.

Step D: Memorize the following Scriptures and have them available in your mind for meditation and motivation to do the will of God.

• "A gentle answer turns away wrath, but a harsh word stirs up anger" (Prov. 15:1, *NASB*).

• "A soothing tongue is a tree of life, but perversion in it crushes the spirit" (Prov. 15:4, *NASB*).

• "Pleasant words are a honeycomb, sweet to the soul and healing to the bones" (Prov. 16:24, *NASB*).